Presented To:

From:

Date:

8 ESSENTIALS
for FOLLOWING
JESUS

8 ESSENTIALS *for* FOLLOWING JESUS

Walk the Walk,
not just
Talk the Talk

Calvin M. Hooper

DESTINY IMAGE® PUBLISHERS, INC.
P.O. Box 310, Shippensburg, PA 17257-0310
"Speaking to the Purposes of God for This Generation and for the Generations to Come."

This book and all other Destiny Image, Revival Press, MercyPlace, Fresh Bread, Destiny Image Fiction, and Treasure House books are available at Christian bookstores and distributors worldwide.

For a U.S. bookstore nearest you, call 1-800-722-6774.
For more information on foreign distributors, call 717-532-3040.
Reach us on the Internet: www.destinyimage.com.

ISBN 13 TP: 978-0-7684-3779-9
ISBN 13 Ebook: 978-0-7684-8996-5

For Worldwide Distribution, Printed in the U.S.A.
1 2 3 4 5 6 7 8 9 10 11 / 13 12 11

Dedication

This book is dedicated to all of those godly soldiers of Christ who have expressed true Christian living before us, even though, to our embarrassment, we may not have been paying attention, and to those who wish to exhibit that kind of life now.

Thank You...

Thank You to God for the inspiration to write this book. It is my prayer that you be blessed and that your Christian walk will be stronger than ever.

Thank you to my beautiful, talented, and anointed wife, Valerie, who is truly a gift from God to me. I love you. Thank you for your encouragement, love, and support throughout the years. You are truly one of a kind. The Bible says he who finds a wife finds a good thing (see Prov. 18:22). You are certainly my good thing! Thanks for always being there.

Thank you to my wonderful children, Calvin II, Jeremy, Natasha, Daisha, and Vincent, for being involved in the ministry. It is such a blessing to see you used by God. I love you! Represent Christ in all you do!

Thank you to my parents, F. M. Hooper and Julia Hooper, as well as my father-in-law, Reuben Sims, and his wife, Jean, for their love and support.

Thank you to Bishop I. V. Hilliard, a man whose example of steadfast devotion to the things of God, love for the people of God, excellence in serving Him, and teaching the Word of God have impacted my ministry in a powerful way. Special thanks to Bishop Charles Wiley who laid the foundation for how I have lived my Christian life since giving my life to Christ many years ago. Special thanks also to Bishop Shelton Bady. Many lessons were learned from you that have impacted me in a very positive way. I appreciate all that I *still* glean from you. Thank God for you!

Finally, thank you to the *greatest church members in the world,* at the Household of Faith Christian Fellowship Church, for your prayers, love, and support. My wife and I are honored to serve you. We love you all!

Contents

Foreword

Pastor's Hooper's book entitled *8 Essentials for Following Jesus* and subtitled *Walk the Walk, Don't Just Talk the Talk* is an insightful, engaging, and instructive discourse that shares the importance of living for God on a daily basis. Pastor Hooper draws from his personal experiences and uses sound biblical principles to convey how essential it is for Christians to live godly lives. The shepherd's heart of Pastor Hooper is warmly felt as he encourages, admonishes, and teaches how and why Christians need to "walk the walk."

This timely message that is being shared by Pastor Hooper is valuable information for new believers who have barely begun to crawl, as well as established and seasoned Christians who can always benefit from edifying words that provoke them to continue on in their walk. Pastors will be able to use this book as an excellent tool to train new members and also as a practical teaching source for Bible studies for all ages.

Wherever you are today in your walk with God, you will be strengthened, encouraged, and blessed as you read and implement the principles and *walk the walk.*

Pastor Geoffrey Stirrup
Dominion COGIC
San Antonio, TX

Introduction

The purpose of this book is to provide you, the Christian, with some key essentials that will serve as the underpinning of a truly transformed, Christlike life. The Bible is clear on how we should live our lives. There are so many distractions, traps, roadblocks, and other things that can get in the way of *living* the Christian life. The key to overcoming these things is to know how to walk the walk.

I do want to make it very clear that this writing is not tied to any denomination whatsoever. There are many great denominational and nondenominational churches in our world, but this writing does not focus on our traditions or our similarities and differences. To be quite frank, we spend far too much time on that anyway and end up displaying attitudes that bring into question what we profess as Christians. This is emphatically a book written for *the Christian*, regardless of your denomination. This book is totally based on what the Bible has outlined for how we are to live our lives.

It is my prayer that once you read this book, your Christian life will perpetually go to higher levels in Christ.

It is my prayer that once you read this book, your Christian life will perpetually go to higher levels in Christ. I do not purport to have given an exhaustive presentation of how a Christian's life should look, but if you apply these essentials, I believe that your life will reflect more of Christ. To God be the glory!

What Is a Disciple?

As I was contemplating the writing of this book, I considered the fact that, in our country, people have so many different ideas as to what a Christian really is. For example, some have the notion that a Christian is someone who goes to church. Although Christians should certainly go to church in accordance with Hebrews 10:25, that is not an exhaustive description of what a Christian is.

Some may say that a Christian is a person who does good deeds and doesn't treat anyone badly. When we read the Bible, we are certainly told that we should treat others the way we would want to be treated (*aka,* the Golden Rule), but the Bible is also very clear that good deeds alone are not the determining factor that qualifies us to be Christian.

The Bible is also very clear that good deeds alone are not the determining factor that qualifies us to be Christian.

Still others say that if we read the Bible then we must be Christians. If that were the case, then anyone who can read would qualify. It is ironic that when you ask people to describe what a doctor is, they don't say, "Oh that is someone who likes to tell people they are sick." Instead they say a doctor is a person who has been through years of medical school to be able to rightfully wear the title *Doctor*. When you think of a soldier, you don't think of it as someone who simply likes military things but as a person who has gone through training and has changed from what he or she was to what he or she is now: a soldier.

As Christians, we are like soldiers. Just like they have to go through training to be transformed into what they are professing to be, we, too, must change in order to truly be the kind of Christians God is calling us to be. First and foremost, a Christian is someone who has been born again. What does being born again mean? It literally means that the life you were living is, in essence, over and a new life has now begun. Whatever sins you committed have been forgiven. You now have a clean slate! You have a new life! Jesus said in John 3:3 that we must be born again. The verse says:

Jesus answered and said to him, "Truly, truly, I say to you, unless one is born again, he cannot see the kingdom of God."

Romans 10:9 tells us how to accomplish that process:

If you confess with your mouth Jesus as Lord, and believe in your heart that God raised Him from the dead, you will be saved.

Once we are born again, the Bible declares in Second Corinthians 5:17 that we are new creations.

Therefore if anyone is in Christ, he is a new creation; old things have passed away; behold, all things have become new (NKJV).

In other words, we must understand that once we are born again, we are now under the leadership of a new master. We used to be slaves to the world and its ways, but now our appetites must change. We must deliberately strive to be more of what God would have us to be and less like the world. The word that sums up what we are to be is *disciple.* That may startle some in our world of eat, drink, and be merry, and yes, this mindset has unfortunately also affected the churches of our society. It seems that people can be more dedicated to their jobs than to their churches. They can be more concerned about me, myself, and I than they are about others.

Have we forgotten what we are really supposed to be doing in this world as Christians? I believe in many regards, we have. We are to be disciples. Jesus told His disciples in Matthew 28:19:

*Go therefore, and make **disciples** of all the nations, baptizing them in the name of the Father and the Son and the Holy Spirit.*

Did you notice what He said? He said make *disciples*. Quite frankly, what has happened in our culture is that the Church has gotten caught up in the *"every church a mega-church" syndrome* and has forsaken fostering discipleship for growing membership. I am certainly not opposed to a church experiencing exponential growth, but when our goal is getting people just for the sake of being large, that is a problem. I'd rather have a church of 1,000 *disciples* than a church of 5,000 members. Why? Because disciples can truly make a difference for the Kingdom.

Jesus never said to go into the entire world and make church members.

Jesus never said to go into the entire world and make church members. He said to make disciples. Yes, we do refer to the people who attend our churches as members, but in too many cases, people who claim to be members are really nothing more than churchgoers. They go to church because it appeases their consciences. They can't imagine not going, because they know they should, but they are not applying the teaching of the Word of God to their lives. Therefore, they have a weekly cycle of conscience-appeasing churchgoing, without any change in their lives.

I must say that the Church has a commitment to its members, as well. That commitment is to teach nothing but the Word of God. It cannot be watered down for the sake of political correctness, the possibility of offending someone, or any other reason. Why? Because the Church is not a political organization. It is a spiritual organism. Also, some people will be offended at times anyway when the light of God's Word shines brightly on their sinful living! If they are offended, praise God! That means the Lord loves them enough to show them the need to change.

**The Church is not a political organization.
It is a spiritual organism.**

I am not advocating that a person should knowingly construct a sermon about another person's wrongdoing. However, as the Word of God is preached, it is inevitable that sometimes the Word will deal with something a person may be doing that is sinful. I know that everyone is at different stages of spiritual growth, but we must understand that our churches must hold fast to the truths of Scripture and purposely promote discipleship so that the people of God can become all they can be. The Church must preach and teach the unadulterated Word of God at all times so that God's people will grow strong spiritually. If your church is teaching the Word of God, consider it a blessing and *apply* what is taught. You will benefit from it. Otherwise, you are just a church-goer too.

When you hear the word *disciple*, what comes to mind? I believe a very accurate definition of the word *disciple* can be found in *Easton's Bible Dictionary*. It says:

> A scholar, sometimes applied to the followers of John the Baptist (Matt. 9:14), and of the Pharisees (22:16), but principally to the followers of Christ. A disciple of Christ is one who (1) believes his doctrine, (2) rests on his sacrifice, (3) imbibes his spirit [to imbibe is to absorb or take in as if by drinking], and (4) imitates his example....[1]

According to W. W. Wiersbe:

> A disciple is a learner, one who attaches himself or herself to a teacher in order to learn a trade or a subject. Perhaps our nearest modern equivalent is "apprentice," one who learns by watching and by doing.

The word *disciple* was the most common name for the followers of Jesus Christ and is used 264 times in the Gospels and the Book of Acts.

Jesus seems to make a distinction between salvation and discipleship. Salvation is open to all who will come by faith, while discipleship is for believers willing to pay a price. Salvation means coming to the cross and trusting Jesus Christ, while discipleship means carrying the cross and following Jesus Christ. Jesus wants as many sinners saved as possible ("that My house may be filled"), but He cautions us not to take discipleship lightly; and He made it clear that there is a price to pay.[2]

Discipleship is a lifelong process of being transformed into the very image of Christ.

We must love Christ more than we love ourselves and our loved ones.

Luke 14:26-27 says:

If anyone comes to Me, and does not hate his own father and mother and wife and children and brothers and sisters, yes, and even his own life, he cannot be My disciple. Whoever does not carry his own cross and come after Me cannot be My disciple.

Wiersbe says:

The word *hate* does not suggest positive antagonism but rather "to love less" (see Gen. 29:30-31; Mal. 1:2-3; and Matt. 10:37). Our love for Christ must be so strong that all other love is like hatred in comparison. In fact, we must hate our own lives and be willing to bear the cross after Him.

What does it mean to "carry the cross"? It means daily identification with Christ in shame, suffering, and surrender to God's will. It means death to self and to our own plans and ambitions and a willingness to serve Him as He directs (see John 12:23-28). A "cross" is something we willingly accept from God as part of His will for our lives.[3]

Matthew 10:24 says:

A disciple is not above his teacher, nor a servant above his master (NKJV).

We have to be submitted and surrendered to our teacher. Ultimately, the Holy Spirit is our teacher. Remember what Jesus said in John 14:26:

But the Helper, the Holy Spirit, whom the Father will send in My name, He will teach you all things, and bring to your remembrance all that I said to you.

The Holy Spirit is our ultimate teacher. He should be allowed to operate in and through us. This brings me to something I call LUI, living under the influence of the Holy Spirit.

Chapter One Review

1. Where is the Scripture that records Jesus saying that we must be born again?

_____

_____

_____

2. How do we become born again? What is the Scripture reference?

_____

_____

_____

3. What is a disciple?

_____

_____

_____

4. Once we are born again, the Bible says we are new creatures. What is the Scripture that supports that?

_____

_____

5. True or False: Discipleship is a temporary process.

_____

_____

6. What does carrying your cross mean?

_____

_____

_____

_____

7. Who is our ultimate teacher? Give the Scripture reference.

_____

_____

_____

8. Are there some areas in your life that are hindering the discipleship process? Take some time to search your heart concerning the matter.

_____

_____

_____

9. Do you love anything more than you love the Lord?

_____

_____

_____

10. Do you consider yourself a disciple? If so, what evidence do you see in your life that indicates you are becoming a disciple?

_____

_____

_____

Endnotes

1. *Easton's Bible Dictionary*, s.v. "disciple," *Biblios. com*, http://eastonsbibledictionary.com/search—disciple (accessed January 27, 2011).

2. W. W. Wiersbe, *The Bible Exposition Commentary an Exposition of the New Testament Comprising the Entire "BE" Series* (Wheaton, IL: Victor Books, 1989), 232.

3. Ibid.

Chapter Two

Living Under the Influence

Before we discuss the eight essentials for living the Christian faith, it is of utmost importance to know that we must be under the influence of the Holy Spirit in order for these eight essentials to manifest in abundance. What does it mean to be under the influence of something? *Influence* can be defined as:

> A power affecting a person, thing, or course of events, especially one that operates without any direct or apparent effort [e.g., being] relaxed under the influence of the music; the influence of television on modern life.[1]

Many people do not have a proper understanding of what being filled with the Holy Spirit means. Let's look at Ephesians 5:18. It says:

And do not be drunk with wine, in which is dissipation; but be filled with the Spirit (NKJV).

As I was studying this verse, I found it interesting that Paul contrasts being filled with wine and being filled with the Spirit. As I was looking at that verse, two questions came to mind. The first question was *What happens to a person under the influence of wine or other alcoholic substance?* The second was *What happens to a person who is under the influence of the Holy Spirit?*

Let me reiterate that an influence can be defined as *"A power affecting a person, thing, or course of events, especially one that operates without any direct or apparent effort...."*[2]

When People Are Under the Influence of Wine...

They do things they would not normally do. Their judgment and perception are impaired. They will commit acts they would not even consider doing while sober. They may think they can fly, but they don't have wings. They'll go places they wouldn't even dare going to if they were in their right mind, but because they are under the influence, they do these things anyway. Most of the time, the results can be devastating.

They say things that they would not normally say. They may be soft-spoken, timid people, but while under the influence of wine, they will say things that are totally out of character. They will talk about your mother, father, brothers, and sisters. They will basically just give you a piece of their minds without any regard for what consequences there may be because they are no longer in control but are under the influence of the alcohol.

The things they do and say are embarrassing to them and others. While under the influence, they don't even realize the amount of embarrassment they are causing themselves and others. Being under this influence has caused jobs to be lost, marriages to be broken, and credibility to be shattered. They are forever viewed by some to be totally out of control and people who no one wants to be bothered with, except those who desire to participate in the same behavior.

The things they do and say are nothing more than the fruit of that "spirit." Wine and other alcoholic beverages are sometimes referred to as spirits. *The American College Heritage Dictionary* defines spirits this way: "an alcoholic beverage, especially distilled liquor."[3] When people partake of spirits, they choose to do so, knowing full well what the potential of the substance is. They enter into the activity with the mindset that they are going to get "full," and when they are, they feel that they can do anything. I'm sure you have heard people use that language before. In fact, you may have been the one who said that yourself before you were born again!

Being under the influence of alcohol can result in headache, sickness, legal issues, loss of your own life or someone else's, and the list could go on and on.

When People Are Under the Influence of the Holy Spirit...

They will do and say things that they would not normally say. Remember Peter? This man Peter is the one who was an unstable leader during the time of Christ, and he even denied knowing Christ when the pressure was on. This same Peter, when under the influence of the Holy Spirit in the Book of Acts, stood up with holy boldness and declared the Word of God! When he did, the Bible says in Acts 2:41 that on *"**that** day there were added about three thousand souls."*

When you are filled with the Holy Spirit, you will declare to a dying world that is lost and trying to find its own way in the darkness that the way has already been made, and it is found in Jesus Christ, who is the way, the truth, and the life! (See John 14:6.) Let me ask the question: How many of you want to be filled with the Holy Spirit? Imagine for a moment a church where *everyone* is filled with the Holy Spirit. That church can impact the world for Christ! *The reason some Christians remain at the same level for so long is because they have not been filled with the Holy Spirit. Why? Because some people don't want to give up themselves for what God has for them. Other things are more important in their lives.*

The reason some Christians remain at the same level for so long is because they have not been filled with the Holy Spirit.

In the world, if you are filled with wine or those other kinds of "spirits" and you attempt to drive an automobile, you may be found guilty of DUI, or driving under the influence. But in the Christian life, we ought to always be found guilty of LUI, or *living under the influence*. In our minds, we ought to be under the influence of the Holy Spirit. In our emotions, we ought to be living under the influence of the Holy Spirit. In our will, we ought to always be living under the influence of the Holy Spirit! Before we allow ourselves to dwell on negative thoughts or say things that would really be better left unsaid, we ought to be influenced by the Holy Spirit. Before we throw our own pity party because we've allowed our emotions to get the best of us, we ought to be influenced by the Holy Spirit. Before we decide that enough is enough and get ready to throw in the towel, we ought to be influenced by the Holy Spirit!

Being under the influence of the Holy Spirit results in having the fruit of the Spirit. It is time for Christians to stop barely getting by, stop always having issues, stop always worrying about everything, and start experiencing the spiritual increase that God has for us. When we are under the influence of the Holy Spirit, we will have love, joy, peace, patience, kindness, goodness, faithfulness, gentleness, and self-control (see Gal. 5:22-23).

Being under the influence of the Holy Spirit has enormous potential. When we are filled with the Holy Spirit, we will have a longing to do all we can for Christ. When Peter was filled, he had a sense of urgency about things; he seized the opportunity to make a difference. He didn't do like some of the modern-day Christians and look to someone else to do it. He didn't say, "Well, I see these people assume that we all are drunk, so since I don't want to offend anyone, I'll wait until next week to address their concerns." He didn't do like he would have done before and join in with the crowd to hide. He was a changed man. He no longer had control; he was now under the influence of the Holy Spirit.

Just as God used him to bring 3,000 souls into the Kingdom, *what can God use you to do if you are filled with His Spirit?* I believe some of you reading this book are looking for God to fill you more with His Spirit. The potential of what God can do when we are filled with His Spirit is limitless. The more we surrender ourselves to the Holy Spirit, the more we are filled with the Holy Spirit. The more we are filled, the more we want to be filled. We crave the righteousness of God. We hate all sin. We want no part of it. We desire to live and walk in the Spirit.

The potential of what God can do when we are filled with His Spirit is limitless.

Paul tells us to live victoriously and to avoid excesses of the flesh (see Phil. 2:12-16). Dwight L. Moody once illustrated this truth as follows:

> "Tell me," he said to his audience, "How can I get the air out of this glass?" One man said, "Suck it out with a pump." Moody replied, "That would create a vacuum and shatter the glass." After many impossible suggestions, Moody smiled, picked up a pitcher of water, and filled the glass. "There," he said, "all the air is now removed." He then went on to show that victory in the Christian life is not by "sucking out a sin here and there," but rather by being filled with the Spirit.[4]

When the Holy Spirit fills us, our lives will be changed, others' lives will be affected, and situations that once seemed to crush us will be seen with a different perspective. As Paul said, I have learned *"in whatsoever state I am, therewith to be content"* (Phil. 4:11 KJV).

When we are under the influence of the Holy Spirit, the things we say and do will not be humiliating and embarrassing. Our words will minister grace to the hearers and our deeds will glorify God. We won't say everything negative that comes to mind when we are under the influence of the Holy Spirit. We won't do any and everything that feels good to us when we are under the influence of the Holy Spirit. Our first priority will be to please God. Paul's use of the imagery of getting drunk with wine is an analogy of doing things the old way and according to the old desires. Living the old way, we aren't concerned about pleasing Him, but living under the influence of the Holy Spirit, pleasing Him is our first priority. We won't want to do anything that brings shame on the name of Christ. We won't want to say or think anything that we would not say or think in the presence of Christ. The Bible tells us to let no filthy communication proceed from our mouths.

Let no unwholesome word proceed from your mouth, but only such a word as is good for edification according to the need of the moment, so that it will give grace to those who hear (Ephesians 4:29).

As we are being filled, we will decrease and Christ will increase in our lives. The Greek word Paul used for the word *filled* in Ephesians 5:18 was *pleroo*. The word means "to fulfill, to make full, and to be filled."[5] We should desire the Holy Spirit to literally saturate our lives.

The next eight chapters will give you eight vital points based on the acrostic *D.I.S.C.I.P.L.E.* These points will continually guide you along the way and help you become a disciple who will be a powerful witness for Christ. These are eight things that I believe should be evident in every Christian. We all are at different levels of growth, but we should be allowing the Holy Spirit to develop these things in us.

Chapter Two Review

1. What does it mean to be under the influence of something?

_____

_____

_____

_____

2. Memorize Ephesians 5:18, and write what it means to you.

_____

_____

_____

_____

3. Why do some people remain at the same spiritual level for so long?

_____

_____

_____

4. True or false: If we are under the influence of the Holy Spirit, we should exhibit the fruit of the Spirit.

_____

_____

5. True or false: If we are under the influence of the Holy Spirit, we won't say much, because we will be more timid.

_____

_____

6. True or false: We have enormous potential when we are filled with the Holy Spirit.

_____

_____

7. True or false: We will usually say things that will embarrass us when we are filled with the Holy Spirit.

_____

_____

8. What should be the first priority in our lives?

_____

_____

_____

9. Is it OK for a Christian to use profanity?

_____

_____

10. What does it mean to be filled with the Spirit?

_____

_____

_____

Endnotes

1. *Your Dictionary.com,* "Dictionary Definitions," s.v. "influence," http://www.yourdictionary. com/influence (accessed October 21, 2010).

2. Ibid.

3. *The American Heritage College Dictionary,* 3rd ed., s.v. "spirit."

4. Paul Lee Tan, *Encyclopedia of 7700 Illustrations: A Treasury of Illustrations, Anecdotes,*

Facts and Quotations for Pastors, Teachers and Christian Workers (Garland TX: Bible Communications, 1996, 1979).

5. James Strong, *The Strongest Strong's Exhaustive Concordance of The Bible* (Grand Rapids, MI: Zondervan, 2001), s.v. "filled" (NT 4137).

Essential One: Discipline Is Necessary

The first letter in our acrostic (D.I.S.C.I.P.L.E.) is "D" for *Discipline.* In Romans 12:1-2, the great apostle Paul wrote:

> *Therefore I urge you, brethren, by the mercies of God, to present your bodies a living and holy sacrifice, acceptable to God, which is your spiritual service of worship. And do not be conformed to this world, but be transformed by the renewing of your mind, so that you may prove what the will of God is, that which is good and acceptable and perfect.*

Disciples understand the magnitude of their callings. They have come to the realization that they are literally vessels of God. Our bodies are the temple of God, and in all that we do, we must allow God to get the glory out of us. First Corinthians 6:19 says:

Or do you not know that your body is a temple of the Holy Spirit who is in you, whom you have from God, and that you are not your own?

Disciples understand that they are no longer their own, but they truly belong to God. Every Christian should strive to be transformed and live for Christ.

The sons of Korah in Psalm 42:1 wrote:

As the deer pants for the water brooks, so my soul pants for You, O God.

Disciples should have a deep longing for the things of God.

Let's look at Psalm 42:1 again. Water is a thirst quencher. When we are thirsty, nothing really quenches that thirst like water. There are substitutes for water, but their goal is to do what water does, and that is to quench thirst. Nothing can replace water. Water sustains life. Have you ever considered the fact that our bodies are over 90 percent water? No matter what we try to use as a substitute, we need a continual supply of water to live.

Just as our bodies need water, our souls need more and more of God. Disciples should have a deep longing for the things of God. That longing causes them to have a steady awareness of God's presence in their lives, and whatever they do, they measure it against God's Word. If it is something that they know will not represent God in a positive manner, they are disciplined enough to refuse to allow themselves to do it. If they are tempted to gossip, they will resist, because the Bible clearly says in Proverbs 20:19:

> *He who goes about as a slanderer reveals secrets, therefore do not associate with a gossip.*

If they are tempted to casually miss church every now and then, they won't because Hebrews 10:25 will remind them:

> *Not forsaking the assembling of ourselves together, as is the manner of some, but exhorting one another, and so much the more as you see the Day approaching* (NKJV).

I will deal more with this verse in the next chapter.

These are just a few examples to illustrate the point that as Christians, we must have discipline. There are many distractions in the world that can cause us to lose our focus, but we must keep in mind that we are just passing through on this earth. Our real business here is doing God's work. That means we have to live lives that are a reflection of Christ and His character. Jesus Christ did not die on the cross so we could pursue lives of sin. He died so that we could be redeemed and have life more abundantly (see John 10:10). We have to see our Christian lives and responsibilities as important and not something we can skimp on.

It is amazing how easy it is for us as Christians to miss a worship service or Bible study and think nothing of it. I am, of course, speaking of those who choose to do so when they know they should be present. Some people have work schedules that prevent them from attending, and some have other legitimate reasons that are understandable, but some have no excuse. It's especially egregious when leaders are not in their proper place. That should never happen. If you are a leader in your church, you *and your family* are called to a higher standard.

We must put God first. He is the One from whom all our blessings flow.

Most of us would dare not miss a day of work every week! Why? We are disciplined to go to work to make money to support our lifestyles. There is one problem, though. We soon forget that it is God who has given us the physical and mental ability to go to the job and our ultimate reward will be given based on our service to Him. We forget that if God had not blessed us, we would not have the ability to work, and therefore, we would not have the house, the car, the groceries, etc.

Too many Christians have their priorities out of order. Rather than seeking God first, they seek other things first. We must put God first. He is the One from whom all our blessings flow. Yes, employment is important. Everyone wants the reward of a paycheck for a job well done. Just as we strive to do well for the earthly paycheck, we should strive even more to do well to please God and receive our eternal reward. The disciplined Christian knows, understands, and lives by the words of Matthew 6:33:

But seek first His kingdom and His righteousness, and all these things will be added to you.

Let me give you an example of something that has happened in my life so you will not think that I am writing about something that I have not done myself. There was a time when I lived about 70 miles away from where I worked. It took me over an hour to get to work and about an hour and thirty minutes to get home. We had Bible studies during the week at 7:00 p.m. on Wednesdays, and I was often responsible for the teaching of class. Even when I was not teaching, my family (my wife and five children) and I were at church when there was a service going on.

As you can imagine, I was tired from getting up early to be at work by 8:00 a.m. at a job *70 miles away,* and fighting through traffic for 90 minutes to get back home and then to church, but I did it because I am dedicated to the cause of Christ. Could I have missed the midweek studies and blame it on the fact that I was tired? The answer is yes. I could certainly have done that, but if I could drive 70 miles to work *five days a week for three years*, I certainly could sacrifice two hours one night a week to be obedient to God and the church leadership He placed me under.

I give you this example not so you can write me and shower me with praise. I humbly share this just to reiterate that discipline is necessary. I sometimes think about what I would be lacking spiritually if I would have taken the easy route and stayed home. The knowledge I gained from being present and accounted for was worth the sacrifice, and it was far less of a sacrifice than driving 70 miles one way to work—and far less of a sacrifice than what Christ did for me.

If we submit to the Holy Spirit and to the Word, we will have no other option but to be disciplined.

Of course, living a disciplined life goes beyond simply going to church. Disciplined living is supposed to govern our treatment of others, our conduct in and out of the presence of others, and everything about us. The governor that controls this is *the Holy Spirit and the Word of*

God. If we submit to the Holy Spirit and to the Word, we will have no other option but to be disciplined.

Remember the deer (see Ps. 42:1). Just as he pants for that water, we have to be disciplined enough that, no matter what, we are going to represent Christ through our lives.

A major part of discipline is guarding your heart. Proverbs 4:23-27 says:

> *Keep your heart with all diligence, for out of it spring the issues of life. Put away from you a deceitful mouth, and put perverse lips far from you. Let your eyes look straight ahead, and your eyelids look right before you. Ponder the path of your feet, and let all your ways be established. Do not turn to the right or the left; remove your foot from evil* (NKJV).

The Book of Proverbs is to the Old Testament what the Book of James is to the New Testament. The book has several main subjects, such as youth and discipline, a good name, business matters, marriage, immorality, wisdom, the tongue, and more. The key word in Proverbs is the word *wisdom.* Proverbs 4:7 says, *"Wisdom is the principal thing; therefore get wisdom. And in all your getting, get understanding"* (NKJV). It's important to note that it is not faith that is mentioned as the principal thing, but it is wisdom. If you have wisdom and understanding of what God is saying to us in His Word, it will lead you to the wise choice to have faith in His Word because you know it to be true. That same wisdom will lead to proper application of God's Word in your life.

A person can have faith and not necessarily have wisdom. In other words, he or she doesn't know or doesn't properly apply the knowledge he or she has. If you do lack wisdom, the Bible tells us in James 1:5 that if we lack wisdom, we should ask God for it. That is very important because the Bible also says that faith without works is dead (see James 2:20,26). That simply means that we have to act on our faith. We have to apply the knowledge we have received. Wisdom tells us how to apply the knowledge we have so that our actions (works) are causing our faith to produce evidence. However, if we lack wisdom, then our actions will hinder our faith. Scripture tells us to guard our hearts. What is the heart, why do we need to guard it, and how do we guard it? Let's examine this more closely so we can gain the wisdom we need.

**If we lack wisdom, then our actions
will hinder our faith.**

So what is the heart? When the Bible talks about the heart, it is not talking about the literal blood-pumping organ in your body. The heart is the innermost center of the natural condition of man. Our heart is often mentioned in Scripture. Jeremiah 17:9 says, *"The heart is deceitful above all things, and desperately wicked; who can know it?"* (NKJV). In Matthew 15:19, Jesus says, *"For out of the heart come evil thoughts, murders, adulteries, fornications, thefts, false witness, slanders."*

The heart is so vital to us that the Bible even lets us know in Romans 10:9 that a change in your heart is necessary for salvation to be received and for you to truly be born again. It says, *"That if you confess with your mouth the Lord Jesus and believe in your heart that God has raised Him from the dead, you will be saved"* (NKJV). The word *believe* implies that there is some kind of change within you that is evidenced by a Christ-centered lifestyle. The ongoing change that results in bad habits being broken, wholesome disciplines being established, and so forth happens faster for some people than for others. Nevertheless, once our heart has been turned over to God, we need to guard it.

The word *believe* implies that there is some kind of change within you that is evidenced by a Christ-centered lifestyle.

That brings us to why we have to guard our hearts. Proverbs 4:23 gives us the clear answer: *"Keep your heart with all diligence, for out of it spring the issues of life"* (NKJV). The condition of your heart determines the condition of your entire life. That's why it must be guarded. If you have a corrupt heart, you live a corrupt life. If you have a righteous heart, you live a righteous life. What does it mean to keep our hearts with all diligence? What are the issues of life? That word *diligence* in the original Hebrew means "guard"[1] or guarding. In other words, out of all the things that you deem precious and of value and worth guarding, the heart should be at the top of the list!

Your heart is the core of your being and is even more important than your physical heart, because the spiritual heart condition will determine your life in eternity. Not only that, but it is the heart that God really cares about. It is out of the heart that the issues of life flow. That word *issues* in the original Hebrew language means "end, limit, starting point."[2] When I saw that definition, I thought about how the heart is where dreams, vision, desire, and passion can end, expand, shrink, or start. I like how Proverbs 4:23 in the Amplified Bible says, *"Keep and guard your heart with all vigilance and **above all that you guard**, for out of it flow the springs of life."* God is not concerned with how proficient you are at making yourself look good on the outside; He is concerned with how proficient you are at keeping yourself looking good on the inside!

The book of First Samuel proves this. We have recorded for us the story of Samuel, Saul, and David. Samuel was a judge in Israel, but when he was old, he appointed his sons as judges over Israel. Samuel was a man who was very dedicated to the Lord, but his sons did not walk in his ways. Therefore, in chapter 8 of First Samuel, we see that the elders of Israel went to Samuel and requested that he give them a king to rule over them so they would be like the other nations around them. The Lord told Samuel to heed to the voice of the people, and although Samuel felt like the people rejected him, the Lord let him know that they really were rejecting Him (see 1 Sam. 8:7).

The Lord sent a message through Samuel to the people warning them of the demands a king would place upon them, but the people still desired a king. How could these people God had already done so much for reject the man of God, God, and the word God sent? It was because of their heart condition. They wanted to be like the other nations around them. They thought they knew what was best for them. They were operating on fleshly emotions rather than on godly wisdom.

Saul was chosen by God as their king. It's interesting that God chose Saul, but I understand why. Because their hearts were turned away from God, the people were caught up in appearances. They had already told Samuel to give them a king so they could be like the other nations, which lets us know that they were looking at what other nations had and were lusting in their hearts to have the same thing. So God gave them a person who fit the ideal appearance of a king. He was taller than anyone else, he was a good-looking guy, and he was sure to be well received by the people. Sadly, Saul was eventually rejected by God as king because of the condition of his heart, which led to his disobedience. When God sent Samuel to anoint the next king, he sent him to the house of Jesse, David's father. When Samuel got there, he saw David's oldest brother, Eliab, and was immediately impressed by his physical stature. Samuel thought that this was surely God's choice based on his appearance and on the physical attributes of the rejected King Saul. But in First Samuel 16:7, we see how God chooses:

> *But the lord said to Samuel, "Do not look at his appearance or at his physical stature, because I have refused him. For the lord does not see as man sees; for man looks at the outward appearance, **but the lord looks at the heart**"* (NKJV).

God's choice became Israel's greatest king. David may not have had the kingly appearance of a person like Saul, but God chose him. God knew his heart was right. In fact, in First Samuel 13:14, Samuel said that God sought a man after his own heart, and the fact that David was chosen means that David was a man after God's own heart. He was not the best choice in man's eyes, but he was the right choice in God's eyes.

Finally, to effectively guard our heart, we need to know how.

**We guard our heart by guarding the
entryways to our heart.**

We guard our heart by guarding the entryways to our heart. What are those entryways? They are the mouth, ear, and eye gates (see Prov. 4:24-27).

I am only dealing with these three gates, but in John Bunyan's book *The Holy War*, he said that there are five gates; he named them the Eye-gate, Ear-gate, Nose-gate, Mouth-gate, and Feel-gate in the city of Mansoul (read "a man's soul").[3] Satan will enter the city of Mansoul through those gates. Bunyan said that we need to stop satan from getting into our hearts through these means. I certainly agree with that. However, I only want to deal with what I believe to be the main gates: the eye, ear, and mouth gates. Keep in mind that the purpose of a gate is to keep unauthorized things out and let authorized things in. If something is trying to enter that is not authorized, shut the gate!

The Mouth Gate (Proverbs 4:24)

"Put away from you a deceitful mouth and put devious speech far from you" (Prov. 4:24).

The eyes and the ears are receivers that affect the heart condition. The mouth is a receiver (receives what is in the heart) and a transmitter (exposes what is in the heart and affects its condition). Therefore, the mouth has great power. It is so great that in James 3:6, he says the tongue can defile the whole body! Remember, the heart is where dreams, vision, desire, and passion can end, expand, shrink, or start. You have to watch what you say. The Bible has much to say about our mouths.

Ephesians 4:29 says, *"Let no corrupt word proceed out of your mouth, but what is good for necessary edification, that it may impart grace to the hearers"* (NKJV).

In other words, if you can't say something useful, don't say anything. Imparting grace means saying whatever needs to be said to help strengthen a person and build him or her up. That's important, because the Bible also says, *"Death and life are in the power of the tongue and those who love it will eat its fruit"* (Prov. 18:21 NKJV).

If our heart is right, then we will speak words that please God and benefit us and others. If our heart is not right, we will speak words that displease God and defile us and add no benefit to others. Jesus said what comes out of the heart defiles the man (see Matt. 15:11).

If we have negative words in queue that we want to release, shut the gate!

The Ear Gate (Proverbs 4:24)

This verse is obviously talking about the mouth, but the ears are also a part of this verse. I particularly want to focus on the second half of the verse: *"and perverse lips put far from thee"* (KJV). What does perverse mean? It means "willfully determined or disposed to go counter to what is expected or desired; contrary."[4] A person with perverse lips is one who will hear the Word go forth and intentionally do opposite of what it said. They'll say things like, "Yeah man, I heard what the pastor said today, but I don't think I need to do that. My life is fine like it is. I don't need to listen to that man; I've got my own relationship with God."

A person with perverse lips is one who will hear the Word go forth and intentionally do opposite of what it said.

I believe that if we have perverse lips, we should certainly apply the Word to ourselves, but I believe this verse also gives us the green light to put away perverse lips of people around us. Remember, the ears are one of the input gates affecting our heart, and we should guard our heart with all diligence above all that we guard! In Proverbs 5, the father gives his son insight on the value of protecting your ears (see Prov. 5:1-4). If you have identified negative input around you, close the gate! It doesn't matter what it may be. It could be gossip, slander, rumors, or unwholesome music; whatever it is, shut the gate and don't let it in!

The Eye Gate (Proverbs 4:25-27)

Job 31:1 says (NIV), *"I made a covenant* ["an agreement, usually formal, between two or more persons to do or not do something specified"[5]] *with my eyes not to look lustfully at a girl."* The eye gate must be protected. It is a receiver that feeds input, whether positive or negative, to the heart. In our society, we are constantly bombarded with images. We don't even have to intentionally look for something unwholesome to look at. It is force fed to us everywhere: in the grocery store line, on television, etc. Even the clothing people purchase in stores now is getting skimpier as the years go by. I told my wife that based on what I see year after year in the stores, she may need to make clothes in the future because there won't be anything in the store decent enough to wear. It doesn't stop there, though. Images of food make us want to go eat things we really don't need. Images of automobiles and other material things make us go out and spend money we really don't have on things we really don't need without us being able to really explain why!

Example of Protecting the Eye Gate

In the summertime, people go to the pool and the beach. Some people ought not to go to the pool or the beach because there's just too much on display and not enough eye gate control.

For example, a man may see a woman, or a boy may see a girl, wearing a swimsuit that looks like it should have been left in the store for someone who could actually fit it. Rather than turning away, he starts gazing at the woman or girl, and at that point a process begins.

The first step of the process is the look. There is an old song that says "just one look is all it took." The second step of the process is the lust (desire to have what you saw). The third step is the temptation (the desire to pursue what you want to have). The final step is sin (obtaining what you want to have). The lust, although sinful, is not the actual act of sin, but it gives birth to it. James 1:14-15 supports this. It says:

But every man is tempted, when he is drawn away of his own lust, and enticed. Then when lust hath conceived, it bringeth forth sin: and sin, when it is finished, bringeth forth death (KJV).

The lust can be avoided if the gate is closed at step one, the look! The problem is that when the gate is left open too long, the process has time to work.

So you may be wondering what we need to have in our heart to keep us living right before God. The answer is very simple. We must hide the Word in our heart. To hide the Word we must:

- Listen to the Word (see Rom. 10:17) (ears)

- Read and study the Word (see 2 Tim. 2:15) (eyes)

- Speak the Word. Death and life are in the power of the tongue (see Prov. 18:21) (mouth)

Psalm 119:11 says, *"Your word I have hidden in my heart, that I might not sin against You"* (NKJV).

It certainly takes discipline to do this. There are some key words in this verse that we need to dissect. First of all, he says he had *hidden* the Word. The word used in Hebrew is *sapan,* which means "treasured or cherished."[6] How many Christians today still treasure the Word of God? Why would he say that he hid the Word? Was he embarrassed by it? Did he not want anyone to know that he knew the Word? The answer, of course, is no. Actually, the fact that he hid the Word is really not that important at all. What is more important is where he hid it.

How many Christians today still treasure the Word of God?

He didn't hide the Word in his head. If so, the Scripture might very well say, "Thy Word have I hidden in my memory bank so I can remember it when necessary." He hid the Word in his *heart.* Why is that an important point? It's important because the heart is the seat of our emotions. The heart is our innermost being. If the Word was hidden in his heart, it would govern everything he did. That also applies to us today. When the Word is in our heart it will govern everything we do. If we understand what the Bible says about the heart, we will understand and seriously strive to hide the Word in our heart. God wants our heart! His Word can redeem, restore, and renew our heart! We must fill our heart with His Word, or we may fall victim to being led by the world's way of being led by our emotions. The world tells us to "follow our hearts" but doesn't tell us where it will lead us. Proverbs 28:26 says, *"He who trusts in his own heart is a fool, but he who walks wisely will be delivered."*

The world has told us that feelings aren't right or wrong, and when listening to someone, we shouldn't argue with their "feelings," because to them, they are real. While this provides an empathetic atmosphere, it can also reinforce satan's work.

The world teaches us that our feelings are the truth. If you "feel" in love, then you should get married. If you feel "out of love," then you should divorce. What is missing in this equation is what the truth is. Our decisions must be based on the truth and not on fleeting feelings that change with the weather, our hormonal levels, or our circumstances. We must be willing to *reject* any feelings that are not consistent with the truth. This is one of the applications of Second Corinthians 10:5, which says, *"taking every thought captive to the obedience of Christ."* How do we know the truth? We know by hiding the Word in our heart. Otherwise we will become polluted with the logic of the world and our lives will look anything but Christian.

The last word to observe in that verse is the word *might*. *"Your word I have hidden in my heart, that I might not sin against You"* (NKJV). There are some who may use that terminology to justify wrongdoing. For example, they may say, "Well the Bible doesn't say that I won't sin; it says that I might not." If a person says that, it is a clear misinterpretation of Scripture and an indication of the misunderstanding of the word *might*. I looked at four different Bible translations, and they all had the word *might* (KJV, NKJV, NLT, NIV). The word *might* does not mean that we have very little chance at living holy and righteous before God. It means exactly the opposite. The word *might* is used to express the possibility. So in essence, that verse is saying, "Your Word have I treasured in my innermost being (heart) in order for it to be possible to not sin against You!" So when I find myself faced with temptation to sin, the more Word I have treasured in my heart, the *greater the possibility* of not choosing to sin!

The more Word I have treasured in my heart, the *greater the possibility* of not choosing to sin!

Keep unauthorized intruders out of your heart. Discipline yourself to only let in those things that have been authorized by the Word of God and your life will be blessed.

Chapter Three Review

1. Which Scripture says we should render ourselves a living sacrifice?

   _____

   _____

2. What does First Corinthians 6:19 mean?

   _____

   _____

3. What should we seek more than anything in our lives?

   _____

   _____

4. Why go to church?

   _____

   _____

   _____

   _____

5. What Scripture encourages us to be consistent in church attendance?

_____

_____

_____

6. Are you more faithful to something than you are to God? Be honest.

_____

_____

_____

7. What are your priorities?

_____

_____

_____

8. What is the heart? What things do you need to rid your heart of?

_____

_____

_____

_____

9. What are some practical ways you can guard the eye gate?

_____

_____

_____

_____

_____

10. What are some practical ways you can guard the ear gate?

_____

_____

_____

_____

_____

11. What are some practical ways you can guard the mouth gate?

_____

_____

_____

_____

_____

Endnotes

1. Biblesoft's New Exhaustive Strong's Numbers and Concordance with Expanded Greek-Hebrew Dictionary. CD-ROM. Biblesoft, Inc. and International Bible Translators, Inc. (1994, 2003, 2006), s.v. "mishmar," (OT 4929).

2. James Strong, *The Strongest Strong's Exhaustive Concordance of The Bible* (Grand Rapids, MI: Zondervan, 2001), s.v. "towtsa'ah," (OT 8444).

3. John Bunyan, *The Holy War* (London: 1682), 9, *Google Books,* http://books.google.com/books?id=wzM7AAAAYAAJ&printsec=frontcover&dq=bunyan+the+holy+war&hl=en&ei=xpdDTcuVMYPQsAOx972LCg&sa=X&oi=book_result&ct=result&resnum=2&ved=0CDEQ6AEwAQ#v=onepage&q=five%20gates&f=false (accessed January 28, 2011).

4. *Dictionary.com,* Dictionary.com Unabridged, Random House, Inc., s.v., "perverse," http://dictionary.reference.com/browse/perverse (accessed January 28, 2011).

5. *Dictionary.com,* Dictionary.com Unabridged, Random House, Inc., s.v., "covenant," http://dictionary.reference.com/browse/covenant (accessed January 28, 2011).

6. James Strong, *The Strongest Strong's Exhaustive Concordance of The Bible* (Grand Rapids, MI: Zondervan, 2001), s.v. "sapan," (OT 6485).

Chapter Four

Essential Two: Involvement Is Needed

The second letter of the acrostic is the letter "I," and it represents *Involvement*. The disciple is a person who is also involved in the things of God. Hebrews 10:25 says:

Not forsaking our own assembling together, as is the habit of some, but encouraging one another; and all the more as you see the day drawing near.

Many people do not understand that their church participation is a vital part of their new life in Christ. Many people treat their church membership as a sort of a country club membership and just go whenever they feel like it. Hebrews 10:25 certainly does not support that notion. Our spirit needs to be constantly fed. We need to purposely get involved in our churches so that we can grow and develop spiritually the way God desires us to do. God did not establish the Church on Earth to be an institution that we casually visit every now and then.

**God did not establish the Church on Earth
to be an institution that we casually visit
every now and then.**

Disciples know that their involvement is important, not just so they can have a clear conscience that they have done their duty by being seen in the number at the local church. They know that their presence is important because they are encouragers to other brothers and sisters. According to the *Bible Exposition Commentary* by Warren Wiersbe:

> It is interesting to note that the emphasis here is not on what a believer *gets from* the assembly, but rather on what he [or she] can *contribute to* the assembly. Faithfulness in church attendance encourages others and provokes them to love and good works.[1]

A disciple never says, *"I'll be there if I can."* A disciple *can't wait* to get to the house of God! Disciples are what we like to call F.A.T. Christians. They are faithful, available, and teachable.

Faithful

You won't have to worry about a disciple being missing in action. Disciples are reliable. Disciples don't miss church for no valid reason. What is an invalid reason? Let me give you a few examples:

1. Oh, I was too tired. (How many of you go to work tired?)

2. My kids took too long getting dressed. (How about planning the night before?)

3. I was sick. (Valid sickness is understandable. I'm talking about people saying they are sick when they have a headache, a cold that isn't contagious, etc.)

Disciples understand that they have an obligation to *God* to be present and accounted for. Disciples understand that their participation is important for themselves and others.

Available

They are qualified and willing to be of service or assistance. Disciples want to be in service to God. Disciples don't run and hide when there is a job to be done. They welcome the opportunity to serve and they do it with Colossians 3:23-24 in mind, which says:

Whatever you do, work at it with all your heart, as working for the Lord, not for men, since you know that you will receive an inheritance from the Lord as a reward... (NIV).

Teachable

Disciples are able and willing to learn. They know they can never learn enough. Once they learn, they are also eager to apply the knowledge in their lives. Disciples welcome instruction, and if they are wrong on a given issue, they welcome correction. Disciples respect leadership. There is an old saying, "If everyone in my church was just like me, what kind of church would this church be?" The answer is rather simple. If you are a faithful, available, and teachable child of God, you have an awesome, healthy, powerful church if everyone is like you! If you are not, there is good news; you can change starting today!

Disciples are able and willing to learn.

If you have a pastor and leaders who are committed to the keeping, teaching, preaching, and living of the Word of God, you will change if you are open and receptive to the teaching. It is such a joy to pastor people who have a desire to obey teaching and to continue to learn more about living the Christian life. It is a tremendous strain to pastor people who always speak negatively against leadership, always have a problem with certain procedures the church may have, always are offended easily about anything and everything, and try to influence others to join in the offense. If you or someone you know talks negatively about the leaders who serve you, cease that kind of behavior today. It is unprofitable for your life. Remember Korah in Numbers 16? Read that as soon as possible. Also read Jude 1:5-13 to see how the New Testament addresses the same attitude. Have a teachable, humble spirit. You'll be much better off as a result.

When it comes to being in the presence of God and other believers, worship is not a chore to the disciple. The disciple has the attitude David had in Psalm 122:1 when he wrote:

I was glad when they said to me, "Let us go to the house of the lord."

Why should you be glad about going to the house of the Lord? Isn't church just an old, boring place with hard seats, bad air conditioning, dull, lifeless people who have no fun, and dry sermons from an old, antiquated book called the Bible that has nothing to do with my life today? I am being facetious here, but the fact is that many people view church this way. Unfortunately, this might describe what your experience with church is actually like. If so, pray for change to come immediately!

On the other hand, some people treat church as a kind of a "go whenever I need a boost" activity where they go to meet their friends and socialize. Learning about the truths of Scripture and how to apply them to their lives is of no concern to them. In fact, they really are doing nothing more than appeasing their own consciences by being at church. They want to avoid the guilt of not being at church on Sunday. To them, "Sunday only" is a good enough strategy. I call these the checking-the-weekly-box Christians. They talk while the pastor is trying to deliver the message. They don't honor God in their giving. In fact, if church goes too long, they leave, even if they got there late and the sermon is still going forth. They can by no means be called disciples.

We should see being in the house of God on Sunday, Wednesday, or whatever days your church has service as *important*, not optional. We should not let anything get in the way of an opportunity to be in corporate worship with other believers. God's Word even tells us not to forsake it (see Heb. 10:25). Now of course, as I have stated already, I am not condemning anyone if you have a work schedule that requires you to work often on days your church has service. In that case, get a copy of the sermon. Get a copy of the Bible study notes. Do whatever it takes to get the teaching!

God has given each and every one of us a gift that must be used for His glory and the advancement of His Kingdom.

We should be involved in our churches. God has given each and every one of us a gift that must be used for His glory and the advancement of His Kingdom. What tends to be the trend, however, is that a few people do all the work that needs to be done in the church. That is a shame. Have you been asked to get involved in an area of your church ministry? Did you willingly accept, or did you find a reason why you couldn't? Many times, we Christians feel like we have to go pray about everything before we get involved. That is not always necessary. Let me give you an example of this in the Bible. Acts 16:9-10 says:

> *A vision appeared to Paul in the night: a man of Macedonia was standing and appealing to him, and saying, "Come over to Macedonia and help us." When he had seen the vision, immediately we sought to go into Macedonia, concluding that God had called us to preach the gospel to them.*

Obviously, Paul shared with them what the Lord had revealed to him. Notice that it did not say they immediately went into a prayer meeting. They believed that Paul was a man of God who heard from God, and they went to get the job done. There was no other revelation they needed to receive from God. *He* saw; *they* went. There are numerous examples of this principle in Scripture. To discuss them all would require the writing of another book. Perhaps that will be a future project. The main point I want to express is that everyone needs to get involved. The Church is a Body, and it takes all the parts doing their part to ease the load on others.

There was no other revelation they needed to receive from God. *He* saw; *they* went.

This is not to say that there are never times when we should pray about getting involved in a particular area of the ministry of our church. We should consider the time commitment and our ability to do a good job serving in a particular area and talk to the pastor or assigned leader to clearly understand the expectations. For example, in a church we were in, the pastor asked for volunteers to run the teen ministry. My wife and I were already involved in other areas of the ministry, but for the sake of the teen ministry, we prayed about it, talked to the pastor about it, and volunteered our services gladly. To God be the glory!

What are some specific involvement areas we all should participate in? I have listed three major areas. Each of these areas could probably have several sub-areas beneath it, but as you get involved in ministry, you will make that determination for yourself.

1. Spiritually—There are souls to be won. Each of us should be trying to lead others to Christ. Each of us should also be praying for each other, our

nation, our leaders, families, schools, the world, etc. We should encourage each other always and restore others in love when they have done wrong. If we are able to teach, we should get involved for the spiritual growth of others. If we can sing or play an instrument, we should use our gifts for God's glory and for the spiritual refreshing of His people. Many opportunities exist for spiritual involvement.

2. Physically—There are certainly plenty of physical-labor tasks that need to be done. Cleaning the church, binding books for classes, making copies, delivering baskets during Thanksgiving, working in the audiovisual ministry, producing copies of sermon CDs, street evangelism and outreach, food service, and the list can go on. There are plenty of opportunities, and the more people who get involved, the better.

3. Financially—Yes, it's true! Churches need finances! It would be great if there were a huge pool of money that we could access to get all we needed with no questions asked, but it does not exist! Jesus spoke about money often. Your church needs your financial support. We need to tithe. We need to give offerings; we need to be guilty of being faithful, consistent, cheerful givers. For those of you who may disagree,

let me ask you this question: If you don't give to the ministry, where is the money going to come from? Furthermore, God delights in people who give faithfully to His work.

Second Corinthians 9:7 says:

Each one must do just as he has purposed in his heart, not grudgingly or under compulsion, for God loves a cheerful giver.

Did you catch that? We should be *glad* about giving financially to God. Our gifts should represent us well. If you have a problem with giving to God, do you also have a problem with God giving to you? Perhaps that question sheds a fresh perspective on the matter. You can never give more to God than He has given to you. You should be eager to show your love and appreciation to God in your giving. When you go to a restaurant, it is customary to leave a tip. That is a way of saying "Thank you" for your service. Has the waiter or waitress done more for you than God? Stop making excuses and start giving cheerfully today. Your church needs your financial support. God gave you what you have anyway, and He promises in His Word to bless you for your obedience.

You can never give more to God than He has given to you.

Get involved in your church. God has gifted you to be used for His glory. Yes, that means you! We all have gifts. I am so blessed when I see the members of our church actively participating. It could be something as simple as taking out the trash, volunteering to come in and assist administratively, or encouraging my wife and me by letting us know that they are praying for us. It all matters a great deal. Romans 12:6-8 says:

> *Since we have gifts that differ according to the grace given to us, each of us is to exercise them accordingly: if prophecy, according to the proportion of his faith; if service, in his serving; or he who teaches, in his teaching; or he who exhorts, in his exhortation; he who gives, with liberality; he who leads, with diligence; he who shows mercy, with cheerfulness.*

In the Body of Christ, we have different gifts that are necessary for the proper functioning of the Body. *Every member of the Body has a ministry,* and every member is called to function in the place appointed by the Lord. It makes no difference who does the work if the glory is his or her own.

> There is a famous story from Sparta. A Spartan king boasted to a visiting king about the walls of Sparta. The visiting king looked around and could see no walls. He said to the Spartan king, "Where are these walls about which you boast so much?" His host

> pointed at his bodyguard of magnificent troops. "These," he said, "are the walls of Sparta, every man a brick."
>
> The point is clear. As long as a brick lies by itself it is useless; it becomes of use only when it is incorporated into a building.[2]

The same principle applies to the individual Christian. To realize his or her destiny, he or she must not remain alone but must be built into the fabric of the local church. Each part constitutes the makeup of one whole.

Every member of the Body has a ministry, and every member is called to function in the place appointed by the Lord.

When you fail to get involved, others are not able to benefit from what God has given to you because you are not allowing God to use you to bless them with your gifts. We all are to help build up the Church.

Chapter Four Review

1. What does F.A.T. stand for?

2. Define what each aspect of F.A.T. means.

_____

_____

_____

_____

3. What are some specific involvement areas we can participate in to help our churches?

_____

_____

_____

4. What aspect of your church ministry are you involved in now?

_____

_____

_____

_____

5. What does Colossians 3:23-24 mean?

_____

_____

_____

_____

6. Do you exhibit what Colossians 3:23-24 says in the things you do? If so, how?

_____

_____

_____

7. True or false: Only certain people who have gifts should do the work of the ministry.

_____

_____

8. True or false: Churches need members to participate in giving financially to the church.

_____

_____

9. True or false: Church attendance should be viewed as important.

_____

_____

10. Are you as involved in your church as you should be?

_____

_____

Endnotes

1. W. W. Wiersbe, *The Bible Exposition Commentary an Exposition of the New Testament Comprising the Entire "BE" Series* (Wheaton, IL: Victor Books, 1989).

2. William Barclay, *The Letters of James and Peter* (Louisville, KY: Westminster John Knox Press, 2003), 226.

Essential Three: Study God's Word

In our D.I.S.C.I.P.L.E. *acrostic,* "S" stands for *Study.* Believe it or not, we all are required to study the Word of God. It is not only the responsibility of the pastor, elders, ministers, and other leaders to study; it is a mandate for all of us.

> *Be diligent to present yourself approved to God as a workman who does not need to be ashamed, accurately handling the word of truth* (2 Timothy 2:15).

To a disciple, the Word of God is more than just another book. Disciples not only hear the Word, but they also *do* the Word. It isn't uncommon for disciples to take notes when the Word of God is being preached and study those notes in their private devotional time so that God's Word will be further engraved upon their hearts. Disciples hide the Word in their hearts. They know that discipleship requires being a student of the Word. They are not easily swayed by false doctrine, because as students of the Word, they are able to easily distinguish truth from error. They are skilled at interpreting the Word in its proper context so that they won't be found guilty of misinterpreting God's precious Word, which would, as a result, bring shame upon them and upon Christ and lead others astray.

Disciples know that discipleship requires being a student of the Word.

An approved worker diligently studies the Word and seeks to apply it to his or her own life. An ashamed worker wastes his or her time with other "religious duties" and has little or nothing to give his or her class or congregation. An approved worker does not waste his or her time arguing about *"words to no profit"* (2 Tim. 2:14 NKJV) because he knows that such arguing only undermines God's work (see 1 Tim. 6:4; Titus 3:9).

An approved workman will shun *"godless chatter"* (2 Tim. 2:16 NIV; 1 Tim. 6:20 NIV), because he knows it only leads to more ungodliness. I fear that some "sharing times" do more harm than good as people exchange their "spiritual ignorance."

It is important to note that Second Timothy 2:15 tells us to study, but we must not miss why it tells us that. It is so we can accurately handle His Word. People who do not take the time to accurately interpret His Word through careful study are setting themselves up for failure. People who take the time to study are what I like to call "dangerous." What does that mean? Simply put, they are serious threats to the devil. They are the people who can intelligently give an answer for why they believe, and in doing this, they can win souls for Christ!

> *But sanctify Christ as Lord in your hearts, always being ready to make a defense to everyone who asks you to give an account for the hope that is in you, yet with gentleness and reverence* (1 Peter 3:15).

They are also the people who, no matter what, are going to stay in the race and not quit because they know that their labor is not in vain!

> *Therefore, my beloved brethren, be steadfast, immovable, always abounding in the work of the Lord, knowing that your toil is not in vain in the Lord* (1 Corinthians 15:58).

Those who don't study are subject to be tossed to and fro because they can not distinguish between truth and error. If we study, we should not be fooled.

> *As a result, we are no longer to be children, tossed here and there by waves and carried about by every wind of doctrine, by the trickery of men, by craftiness in deceitful scheming* (Ephesians 4:14).

Studying God's Word is essential to spiritual growth. Perhaps you don't know how to study. Here is a basic method you should use that will cause you to dig deeper into the Word of God. It is a simple method known as the five Ws and an H. The five Ws are: who, what, when, where, and why. The H is how. When reading a passage of Scripture, in order to get the meaning out of it (also known as *exegesis*) or extracting from the Word the meaning that is actually there, you must ask these questions. For example, let's take Psalm 23:1-3, which says:

> *The lord is my shepherd, I shall not want. He makes me lie down in green pastures; He leads me beside quiet waters. He restores my soul; He guides me in the paths of righteousness for His name's sake.*

When you apply the five Ws and an H, you can come up with questions like: Who is the Lord? What does a shepherd do? Where does He lead me? How does He guide me? And so on. This is a quick example just to get you started.

There are great tools out there to assist you with studying the Word of God. Any good Christian bookstore should have them. Mardel, Family Christian Store, and Lifeway are three excellent sources to help build up your Christian book library. At a minimum, you should have a good study Bible. The *Life Application Study Bible* (New American Standard Bible Updated Edition, published by Zondervan) is one I use often. I also have the

Archaeological Study Bible (published by Zondervan) and others. Study Bibles have additional helps in them to give you a better understanding of the Scriptures. You should also have a good Bible dictionary and a concordance, because the dictionary will give you quick access to detailed information on people, places, things, etc. The concordance will help you dig deeper into the meaning of Scripture by defining the original Hebrew and Greek words from which our Scriptures were translated. There are also some excellent online sites for reliable Bible study. You will have to pray for discernment on which ones are best to use, or consult your Pastor if you are unsure. Here's a short list for you to start with:

www.intothyword.org

www.biblestudytools.com

www.blueletterbible.com

www.internationallegacy.org

In our country, many people suffer from a very sad ailment called *spiritual illiteracy*.

I find it interesting that people expect doctors to have studied in order to know how to diagnose you correctly and use the tools of their trade. Lawyers are expected to know the law in order to represent their clients. Soldiers are expected to know how to use their weapons and tactics in order to be successful on the battlefield. Christians should be expected to know the Word of God and how to apply it to their lives in order to be successful as well. You should expect that of yourself. If we are Christians, we need to know our Word! In our country, many people suffer from a very sad ailment called *spiritual illiteracy*. There are three key ways to avoid this.

- First of all, be involved in the corporate Bible study times in your church. This is when Bible study takes place among all the members together. Perhaps your church has a different format, but the main thing I want to express is that if your church has some form of biblical teaching, go to it. Sunday morning sermons should be biblical too, but at our church, for example, we go into a plethora of subjects on Wednesday nights such as world religions, spiritual warfare, prayer and fasting, pneumatology (study of the Holy Spirit), and much more. Members are encouraged to ask questions and have discussion to get a firm understanding. There are PowerPoint presentations, and sometimes video is used to help teach as well.

- Second, carve out a dedicated personal time to study the Word. This is a crucial practice. You must get personal time in the Word of God.

- Third, when there is a service at church, whether it is worship, Bible study, men's or women's group study, marriage enrichment, a conference, revival, etc., *get to the church*! The church is your training center!

Of course, there are times when you will miss church or study due to work, or perhaps you are out of town or legitimately need to stay home sick. What does legitimately being sick mean? Basically, if you are clear to go to your job under the weather a bit, you should make that same push to get to church. I know I have done that myself unless I have been deemed contagious. In that case, I didn't go to church or work. Christians have got to have a paradigm shift, which is simply a change in how they think. Your job or business is not what you should live your life for. You should live your life to please God.

Whatever you do, do your work heartily, as for the Lord rather than for men (Colossians 3:23).

Whatever you have to do in order to keep feeding yourself on the Word of God, then do it. Proverbs 4:7 says:

The beginning of wisdom is: Acquire wisdom; and with all your acquiring, get understanding.

So you might say, "What is wisdom?" Wisdom is the something that enables us to use knowledge rightly. Wisdom resists group pressures, thinks for itself, and is reconciled to the use of its own judgment.[1]

Wisdom is the something that enables us to use knowledge rightly.[2]

God desires for His people to be wise. James 1:5 tells us, *"If any of you lacks wisdom, let him ask of God, who gives to all generously and without reproach, and it will be given to him."* James is not talking about simply having knowledge; he is talking about the ability to make wise decisions in the circumstances of life. Another term for wisdom is *practical discernment.* It first begins with respect for God, leads us to right living, and results in us having an increased ability to tell the difference between right and wrong. Many Christians grope around in the dark hoping to somehow stumble across answers. This is most unnecessary, because all we have to do is pray to God for Him to grant us wisdom, read His Word so that we will know His will, and ask Him to show us how to obey it.

We will do all we can to get to work, no matter what the weather is or how we are feeling that day, so we can make that money. We should have that same attitude when it comes to our spiritual development. How much more valuable is your relationship with God? I pray that you are in a good, solid, Bible-teaching, Bible-believing, and Bible-*living* church where you can grow, fellowship, and be used by God. Your church will not be perfect, because none of us are perfect people. However, it should strive to teach, believe, and live the truths of God's Word.

The world needs Christians who are equipped with the knowledge of the Word of God. There are so many counterfeits out there, and God needs us to help people believe the truth. Too many people are being deceived by the devil's lies. Imagine what your church would be like if everyone had a hunger for the knowledge of God's Word! We need to have a real passion for the Word of God!

I read an illustration that beautifully relays the message of how badly we should hunger for more of God's Word:

> A young man came to Socrates one day and said, in substance: "Mr. Socrates, I have come 1,500 miles to gain wisdom and learning. I want learning, so I come to you."
>
> Socrates said, "Come, follow me." He led the way down to the seashore. They waded out into the water until they were up to their waists, and then Socrates seized his companion and forced his head under the water. In spite of his struggles, Socrates held him under.
>
> Finally, when most of his resistance was gone Socrates laid him out on the shore and returned to the marketplace. When the visitor had regained his strength, he returned to Socrates to learn the reason for this behavior.

Socrates said to him, "When you were under the water, what was the one thing you wanted more than anything else?"

"I wanted air."

Then Socrates said, "When you want knowledge and understanding as badly as you wanted air, you won't have to ask anyone to give it to you."[3]

In an earlier chapter, I referenced Romans 12:1-2, which says:

I beseech you therefore, brethren, by the mercies of God, that you present your bodies a living sacrifice, holy, acceptable to God, which is your reasonable service.

And do not be conformed to this world, but be transformed by the renewing of your mind, that you may prove what is that good and acceptable and perfect will of God (NKJV).

The objective of study is to gain an understanding of Scripture.

The objective of study is to gain an understanding of Scripture. Gaining that understanding, and applying it, is critical to your transformation. As I thought about this, I wrote ten things I believe should be characteristic of a person who has a right understanding about God in his or her life. Using the acrostic U.N.D.E.R.S.T.A.N.D., you will:

1. *Use the Word of God in your life* (see James 1:23-25). James says we should be doers and not hearers only. When we have a right understanding of God, we will find ourselves applying what He says rather than just hearing and taking no action.

2. *Not faint* (see Gal. 6:9). We won't allow ourselves to quit on God when we have the understanding that serving and obeying Him has rewards that are not always revealed immediately.

3. *Desire more of God* (see Ps. 42:1). Just as a deer thirsts for the water brook, we should desire more of God when we realize that He is what we need to satisfy us spiritually, just like the water is refreshing to the deer.

4. *Enjoy God.* The psalmist says, *"I will bless the lord at all times; His praise shall continually be in my mouth"* (Ps. 34:1 NKJV). When we understand God, we will not have a problem enjoying His presence, enjoying serving Him, worshiping Him, and living for Him.

5. *Reverence God.* Ecclesiastes 12:13 says to *"Fear God and keep His commandments, for this is the whole duty of man"* (NIV). We should have such an understanding that we realize that no matter what we accomplish in life, no matter how much wealth we have accumulated, no matter what kind of connections we might have, it all amounts to nothing if God is not reverenced!

6. *Seek God.* Colossians 3:1 says, *"Therefore if you have been raised up with Christ, keep seeking the things above...."* To seek God means to put Heaven's priorities into practice daily.

7. *(Be) Thankful unto God* (see Col. 3:15). Be thankful for what God has done in your life.

8. *Accept what He allows.* Deuteronomy 4:39 says, *"Know therefore today, and take it to your heart, that the lord, He is God in heaven above and on the earth below; there is no other."* We won't always understand why God allows some of the more difficult things in our lives to happen. But we can be sure that He knows what is best for us, and all things are working together for good for those who love God and are called according to His purpose (see Rom. 8:28). Things happen to some people because of their own error.

There are times in life when we will have to endure hardness as good soldiers of Jesus Christ.

---

9. *(Develop a) "Nevertheless" type of attitude* (see Mark 14:36 NKJV). Jesus showed us what having a nevertheless attitude looks like when He cried out in Mark 14:36, *"Abba, Father, all things are possible for You. Take this cup away from Me;* **nevertheless,** *not what I will, but what You will"* (NKJV). There are times in life when we will have to endure hardness as good soldiers of Jesus Christ. Christ endured the ultimate sacrifice for us and in the process showed us what kind of attitude a person ought to have when he or she has a right understanding of God. We have to have that same mental fortitude. We have to have that "nevertheless" toughness! We have to be able to say, "God, I know that serving You means there are some things I must give up. Nevertheless, I will because the reward I will gain is greater than what I have to lose. God, I know that I'm not perfect. I know I've made some mistakes, and I don't see how You can use me to Your glory. Nevertheless, here I am, Lord. Use me as You will!" We have to be able to say, "God, You said walk by faith and not by sight, (see 2 Cor. 5:7) and I can't see the way clearly. Nevertheless,

I'm going to trust You. I'm going to obey You. I'm going to serve You, nevertheless!"

10. *Devote yourself to Him* (see Rom. 12:1-2). In all that we do, we should give God all the glory and honor that is due unto Him.

Are these qualities evident in your life? Is your mind still the same as it was before you were born again? If so, a renewal needs to take place, and it will by studying and conforming to the Word of God. The changes probably won't all happen at one time, which is why discipleship must be a lifelong process.

Study the Word of God. Your life and others' lives will be changed as a result.

Chapter Five Review

1. What are three basic things you can do to prevent spiritual illiteracy?

   _____

   _____

   _____

2. What is the important principle expressed by Colossians 3:23?

   _____

_____

3. What are the five Ws and an H?

_____

_____

4. True or false: Disciples don't do the Word; they just have knowledge of it.

_____

_____

5. Name the Scripture that tells us to study the Word of God.

_____

_____

6. According to this Scripture, why do we study?

_____

_____

_____

7. What are ten things that should be characteristic of a person who has a right understanding of God as a result of studying the Word of God?

_____

_____

8. Do you exhibit these ten characteristics? If not, which areas need improvement?

Endnotes

1. Pastor's Library Software, Logos Bible Software version of P. L. Tan, *Encyclopedia of 7,700 Illustrations* (Garland TX: Bible Communications, 1996).

2. Ibid.

3. Ibid.

Essential Four: Commitment Is Vital

We're already on the "C" in our acrostic, which stands for *Commitment*. God expects us to be committed to Him. Philippians 3:8-14 says:

> *More than that, I count all things to be loss in view of the surpassing value of knowing Christ Jesus my Lord, for whom I have suffered the loss of all things, and count them but rubbish so that I may gain Christ, and may be found in Him, not having a righteousness of my own derived from the Law, but that which is through faith in Christ, the righteousness which comes from God on the basis of faith, that I may know Him and the power of His resurrection and the fellowship of His sufferings, being conformed to His death; in order that I may attain to the resurrection from the dead. Not that I have already obtained it or have already become perfect, but I press on so*

that I may lay hold of that for which also I was laid hold of by Christ Jesus. Brethren, I do not regard myself as having laid hold of it yet; but one thing I do: forgetting what lies behind and reaching forward to what lies ahead, I press on toward the goal for the prize of the upward call of God in Christ Jesus.

Paul was a man who certainly had impressive credentials. In the preceding verses, he is not boasting. He is actually making a point that he has done nothing that could be considered more important, nobler, and more vital to his life than his relationship to Christ. He would willingly give up all the accolades and accomplishments for Christ, and in essence, he had done just that. Before Christ, he was committed to things he considered to make him righteous, but now nothing was more important than Christ. His example of commitment is one that we all should have if we want to become disciples!

His example of commitment is one that we all should have if we want to become disciples!

Warren Wiersbe made a great point when he said:

The Christian life is not a game; it is a race that demands the very best that is in us. Too many Christians live divided lives. One part enjoys the things of the world, and the other part tries to live for the Lord. They get ambitious for "things" and start minding earthly ambitions. Our calling is a "high calling" and a "heavenly calling"; and if we live for this world, we lose the prize that goes with our high calling.[1]

God is not content with being our part-time Lord. In First Samuel 7:3, when Samuel addressed the house of Israel, he said:

If you return to the lord with all your heart, remove the foreign gods and the Ashtaroth from among you and direct your hearts to the lord and serve Him alone; and He will deliver you from the hands of the Philistines.

Just as Samuel addressed them then, we too must take an introspective look at exactly what holds first priority in our lives. If God is competing for first place with anything else in your life, then He is not truly Lord of your life. The Israelites knew who God was, but over the course of time, they allowed other things to capture their focus. God is either Lord of all or He is not Lord at all. Some of us may have allowed other gods to come in and capture our focus. It could be money, worry, doubt, material things, etc. God deserves our undivided attention! If He knows the number of hairs on our heads, surely He knows how to provide for us. Our responsibility is to put our faith and trust completely in Him and not waver, knowing that what God has promised He is also able to perform (see Rom. 4:21). It is time to remove the gods that come and steal some of our service away from the one true and living God!

Surely there will be times in your life when you may be afraid, unsure, and doubtful. I'm sure that the Israelites faced the same thing, but they removed the gods and experienced victory, restoration, and peace. When we put God first and serve Him with an undivided heart, we too will experience the blessing that they did.

God is either Lord of all or He is not Lord at all.

Unfortunately, many, even Christians, do not know what commitment looks like because of the lack of commitment we see every day. A perfect example is the lack of commitment to marriage. Our marriage relationships and our relationships with God are very much alike. Look what Paul said in Ephesians 5:25-32:

> *Husbands, love your wives, just as Christ also loved the church and gave Himself up for her, so that He might sanctify her, having cleansed her by the washing of water with the word, that He might present to Himself the church in all her glory, having no spot or wrinkle or any such thing; but that she would be holy and blameless. So husbands ought also to love their own wives as their own bodies. He who*

loves his own wife loves himself; for no one ever hated
his own flesh, but nourishes and cherishes it, just as
Christ also does the church, because we are members
of His body. FOR THIS REASON A MAN SHALL
LEAVE HIS FATHER AND MOTHER AND
SHALL BE JOINED TO HIS WIFE, AND THE
TWO SHALL BECOME ONE FLESH. This
mystery is great; but I am speaking with reference to
Christ and the church.

It can obviously be seen in this passage that the marriage relationship requires commitment. Our relationship with Christ requires that same kind of commitment. Marriage is the perfect relationship to illustrate how we, the Bride of Christ, are connected to Him and how we are to relate to one another. As the Bride of Christ, we, being many imperfect people, are to be *one* body, and we are connected to Christ who is, of course, perfect. Collectively we are the cells that make up the composition of the Bride that Christ will one day come to receive to Himself. It is a marvelous thing how all of us, who were worthy of everlasting punishment, have been given a second chance and have been allowed to be a part of this great Bride known as the Church. I believe that we may in fact take for granted how special our relationship to God and one another really is, but let me illustrate it this way.

Many visitors to Ireland bring home some of the famous Waterford crystal. It's very expensive. Every piece is perfect. Often a person may buy fine china or crystal at bargain prices if that person is willing to accept an imperfect piece, "a second." But there are no "seconds" in Waterford crystal. If a piece has the slightest imperfection, it is crushed, melted, and made over entirely. The Church, however, is completely made up of "seconds." The Church is filled with imperfect people who have all been forgiven by the grace of God. In marriage, we must remember that neither of us is perfect! Likewise, in the Church, we must remember that none of us is perfect. We are all seconds. We all have imperfections. Even with our imperfections, Christ calls us His Bride.

The Church is filled with imperfect people who have all been forgiven by the grace of God.

What we see happening, though, is that when a person's marriage doesn't go according to the unrealistic expectations they entered the relationship with, they bail out! In fact, some even make provisions for failure before the marriage. That's called the prenuptial agreement. Why is there such a lack of commitment? Because of selfishness that abounds in our country. The media would lead you to believe that life is all about you. If you aren't happy with your spouse, just throw him or her away (divorce), and start over! What a sad story. What's worse is that divorce is just as common in the Church as it is out of the Church. The key to changing that is to teach the uncompromised Word of God.

There are, of course, biblical reasons for divorce, although we do not have to exercise those options, and I am in no way saying that if you have experienced divorce in your life there something is wrong with you. However, in our society today, more commitment to God would lessen the rate of divorce. I speak from experience. My wife and I went through a very difficult time in our relationship. I was a widower with three kids, and she was a single mother of one. There were adjustments to be made that were not made, and trouble ensued. I won't go into the details of all that occurred, but at one point, I was ready to divorce! It was nothing but our commitment to God and love for each other that held everything together and caused us to reconcile, and now our marriage is better than ever. If we had divorced, it would have been a terrible mistake.

The same thing applies to our relationship with God. When people feel that God has let them down, or things don't go their way, they bail out. They look for other avenues to satisfy themselves. It may be sex, drugs, gambling, etc., none of which can ever replace a relationship with God. I believe that this lack of commitment can be attributed to a lack of knowledge. God's people are simply not studying the Word of God the way they should. Commitment to God will make it harder for us to transgress against Him.

Commitment to God will make it harder for us to transgress against Him.

We won't gossip when opportunity comes; we won't have a critical spirit of people; we won't think we are always right and never receive correction that is for our own good, etc. My wife and I once told a teen study group that if you do all you can to truly learn the Word of God, it will be so much harder to deliberately sin against Him! That's why the psalmist David said in Psalm 119:11:

Your word I have treasured in my heart, that I may not sin against You.

In my humble opinion, if you are disciplined, involved, and studious, commitment will be a natural by-product because you have come to truly know God and His faithfulness through His Word. You may go through tough times, but you'll stay committed because you know that His Word says the following in Psalm 37:5-9:

Commit your way to the lord, trust also in Him, and He will do it. He will bring forth your righteousness as the light and your judgment as the noonday. Rest in the lord and wait patiently for Him; do not fret because of him who prospers in his way, because of the man who carries out wicked schemes. Cease from anger and forsake wrath; do not fret; it leads only to evildoing. For evildoers will be cut off, but those who wait for the lord, they will inherit the land.

Stay committed to God. Your eternal reward will be so much greater than any temporary reward the world can ever provide. Your commitment to God is not in vain. The devil will surely tempt you, but when you know God's Word, you will be able to stand. Jesus gave us an example of how to deal with the devil's temptation in Matthew 4:2-11. It says:

And after He had fasted forty days and forty nights, He then became hungry. And the tempter came and said to Him, "If You are the Son of God, command that these stones become bread." But He answered and said, "It is written, 'MAN SHALL NOT LIVE ON BREAD ALONE, BUT ON EVERY WORD THAT PROCEEDS OUT OF THE MOUTH OF GOD.'" Then the devil took Him into the holy city and had Him stand on the pinnacle of the temple, and said to Him, "If You are the Son of God, throw Yourself down; for it is written, 'HE WILL COMMAND HIS ANGELS CONCERNING YOU'; and 'ON their HANDS THEY WILL BEAR YOU UP, SO THAT YOU WILL NOT STRIKE YOUR FOOT AGAINST A STONE.'" Jesus said to him, "On the other hand, it is written, 'YOU SHALL NOT PUT THE LORD YOUR GOD TO THE TEST.'" Again, the devil took Him to a very

*high mountain and showed Him all the kingdoms of
the world and their glory; and he said to Him, "All
these things I will give You, if You fall down and
worship me." Then Jesus said to him, "Go, Satan!
For it is written, 'YOU SHALL WORSHIP THE
LORD YOUR GOD, AND SERVE HIM ONLY.'"
Then the devil left Him; and behold, angels came
and began to minister to Him.*

God's Word will see us through, if we have faith in
Him. Sometimes we may fall, but we can get back up
again. First John 1:9 gives us that assurance. Commitment, I believe, means that we are 100 percent sold out to
Christ and the life that we are instructed to live according
to the Word of God. This does not mean we will attain
perfection, because none of us is perfect. Romans 3:23
dispels the notion of perfection when it says:

For all have sinned and fall short of the glory of God,

I believe a key word in this verse is *have.* It says that
we *have* sinned, not that we are sinning. It is true that
even after we are saved, we must deal with our sin na-
ture, and we will make some mistakes and need to repent.
However, too many Christians use this verse as an excuse
for doing wrong. Once you have confessed Christ as your
Lord according to Romans 10:9, you should be striving
daily to live a life of holiness and righteousness.

**Once you have confessed Christ as your Lord...
you should be striving daily to live a life of
holiness and righteousness.**

The term is called *sanctification*. Once we are saved, we are positionally sanctified or set apart for God; but after that is where our commitment comes into play. That is called *progressive sanctification*. Faithful church attendance, personal Bible study, Bible study at your local church, and the deliberate application of the Word of God to your life all contribute to us becoming more and more Christlike. That is what God wants, and it's what all Christians should do. The good news is that we are not alone in this endeavor, for the Bible says in Philippians 4:13:

I can do all things through Christ who strengthens me (NKJV).

That verse totally obliterates any excuse we may conjure up for why we can't live our lives like God's Word prescribes. You may say you can't do it, but God's Word says you can!

I believe that many times it really isn't that we can't be committed, but we just don't do it. The reason, I believe, is very simple. Our understanding is lacking. Once we give our lives to Christ, we belong to Him! We have an obligation to glorify God in our bodies and spirit.

Do you not know that your body is a temple of the Holy Spirit who is in you, whom you have from God, and that you are not your own? For you have been bought with a price: therefore glorify God in your body (1 Corinthians 6:19-20).

If you get in your car and the car says to you, "I'm not working today. I'm on vacation. Please find another ride," would you be happy about that? Would you accept it? No, of course not. Why? The car belongs to you. It is not its own! Likewise, since we are no longer our own when we become Christians, how do you think God must feel when we give Him excuses for why we can't serve Him after all He has done for us? Here's an exercise for you. Take out a sheet of paper and write down all the valid reasons why we should not serve God. That sounds ludicrous, doesn't it? How do you think our excuses sound to Him?

Finally, our commitment requires a changed mind. Romans 12:2 says:

And do not be conformed to this world, but be transformed by the renewing of your mind, so that you may prove what the will of God is, that which is good and acceptable and perfect.

In case you have not been paying attention, the world we live in is messed up spiritually! The world has many methods for changing the mind, none of which has God's seal of approval. As a Christian, you cannot commit to the world's way of thinking. The world may say it is necessary to read your horoscope every day. The world says you need to have good karma. The world may say that in order to become rich, you should play the lottery often because you never know! The world would say that you should live with someone before you marry him or her. After all, don't you have to try things out to make sure you're going to like it? First Corinthians 3:19 says:

> *For the wisdom of this world is foolishness before God. For it is written, "He is THE ONE WHO CATCHES THE WISE IN THEIR CRAFTINESS."*

If our minds are changed from thinking the world's way to thinking God's way, not only will our commitment be strong, but it also will not even be a consideration to do anything other than serve the Lord, knowing that when this life is over, we shall have a greater reward than anything we could ever receive in this life.

Chapter Six Review

1. First Samuel 7:3 mentions foreign gods. What are some examples of the foreign gods that people allow themselves to devote more attention to?

   _____

   _____

2. According to First Corinthians 6:19-20, why should you be committed to God?

_____

_____

3. What Scripture indicates to us the need for a changed mind in order to have commitment to God?

_____

_____

_____

4. Memorize Psalm 119:11 and put it into practice.

5. What weapon did Jesus use every time satan tempted Him in Matthew 4:2-11?

_____

_____

_____

6. Based on Jesus' example, we need to know the Word of God. Do you have a prayer time you commit to? Do you study the Word? Are you active in Bible study at your church if your schedule allows?

_____

_____

_____

7. List some areas in your life that hinder your commitment to God (e.g., slothfulness, procrastination, laziness, bad relationships, etc.) Pray for God to help you in these areas as you strive to become more like Christ.

_____

_____

_____

Endnote

1. W. W. Wiersbe, *Wiersbe's Expository Outlines on the New Testament* (Wheaton, IL: Victor Books, 1997), s.v. "Phil. 3:1."

Essential Five: Integrity

Now for the second "I" in our acrostic: *Integrity.* The very mention of the word *integrity* invokes a certain fear in a person. It causes one to somewhat self-evaluate to see whether one's life is worthy of being called full of integrity.

> **Once you have truly gotten serious about the things of God, integrity will be something that will be of major importance to you...**

Integrity raises the bar. Therefore, many will compromise, feeling as if they are not able to clear the bar of integrity at all times. I find it interesting that we will push ourselves to accomplish great things on our jobs and at everything else we want to do.

It does not matter how high the bar is for some, they will do *what they need to* in order to meet that standard.

However, when it comes to God, they lose that zeal and drive. They'll say things like, "It doesn't take all of that." This is really inexcusable. Perhaps at some point in their lives, integrity was a weakness for them, but once you have truly gotten serious about the things of God, integrity will be something that will be of major importance to you, because our representation of Christ is something that the world needs, and integrity is what makes that representation shine bright. Paul wanted to know Christ; he wanted to be like Him. He wanted to be all that Christ wanted him to be. So, what is integrity? According to *The American Heritage College Dictionary,* integrity is:

> Steadfast adherence to a strict ethical code... the state of being unimpaired; soundness... the quality or condition of being whole or undivided; completeness.[1]

Therefore, my beloved brethren, be steadfast, immovable, always abounding in the work of the Lord, knowing that your toil is not in vain in the Lord (1 Corinthians 15:58).

There are three key words to take note of here.

1. Steadfast—"unwavering or determined in purpose, loyalty, etc...."[2]

2. Immovable—"...not intended to be moved."[3] "... incapable of being moved; fixed; stationary...."[4]

3. Abounding—"to occur or exist in great quantities or numbers...."[5]

Although I have read First Corinthians 15:58 several times, I saw that in this verse Paul is not double-talking when he says to be steadfast and immoveable. To be steadfast is referring to the *state of mind that a disciple must have*. As a result of having a made up our minds, we will be immovable. In other words, no matter what, it will not be possible to be moved from the faith that you know you possess! A disciple understands that to abound is to continue to do good regardless of whether or not results are immediately seen. Disciples don't just live for the moment, but they maintain a heavenly perspective, knowing that what they do for Christ will have eternal results. Because of Christ, victory is ours! Romans 8:37-39 tells us:

> *But in all these things we overwhelmingly conquer through Him who loved us. For I am convinced that neither death, nor life, nor angels, nor principalities, nor things present, nor things to come, nor powers, nor height, nor depth, nor any other created thing, will be able to separate us from the love of God, which is in Christ Jesus our Lord.*

In our society, we require integrity of many people, often without even realizing it. Let's look at the definition of integrity again:

Steadfast adherence to a strict ethical code…
the state of being unimpaired; soundness…
the quality or condition of being whole or
undivided; completeness.[6]

Can you think of anyone you hold to this standard?
Here's one example I thought of that we all can probably identify with. When you go to the doctor, you probably expect him or her to know how to properly diagnose
you and what treatment to prescribe for you. This is why
we say that doctors "practice" medicine or that lawyers
"practice" law, etc. One of the definitions for practice is
"to perform or do repeatedly in order to acquire skill or
proficiency…."[7] What if you went to the family doctor
for a sore throat and he told you that he really wasn't sure
what to do? What if he came into the examination room
with obviously dirty hands? What if he just made fun of
your sickness and then prescribed something that was not
designed to treat your specific illness at all? Would you
say that doctor was one who had integrity?

The answer is obvious. This is just one example. Just
like we expect a certain behavior or skill level out of doctors or other professionals, God expects the same out
of Christians. In the example of the doctor, there were
some things that should and should not have been done.
He should have known what to do for the sore throat.
He should have cleaned his hands before seeing you. He
should not have made fun of the sickness, and he should

not have prescribed the wrong thing. We expect integrity from the doctor. We expect that the right thing will be done in our presence or absent from us. I know that even doctors make mistakes, but I was overly dramatic in this illustration for the purpose of driving home the point.

People expect us to be *Christlike*. More importantly, we should desire to be Christlike.

The same principle applies to Christians. People expect us to be *Christlike*. More importantly, we should desire to be Christlike. We should be able to help people. If someone comes to you at work and says, "Please pray for me," he or she is not wanting you to wait until you get to church next Sunday; he or she needs and wants prayer now! Stop and take the time to pray for the person right there. If you need to go into a conference room, step in the hallway, or go outside, do it! Meet people's needs right where they are! You don't know what may happen to them before you get the chance to go to church and pray for them.

We should strive to represent Christ always in our lives. We should love people regardless of who they are or what they may be doing that is contrary to the Word of God. We have to always remember that God loves all people. He loves people you might classify as unlovable: the drunk, prostitute, adulterer, embezzler, liar, pimp, stubborn, arrogant, etc. The list can go on and on. He never hates people; He hates sin, *and so should we.* If we can remember that what ails people is sin, we can properly usher them into what will cure them, and that is a relationship with Jesus Christ. Remember, it's not the person we should hate but the sin.

We should not make compromises for sinful behavior, either. We should help people overcome it. We too will make mistakes sometimes, but if we practice our Christianity daily, our skill at living the life will become polished, any knowledge we lack will be acquired, and our integrity will not be questioned because we will reflect Christ. In my example of the doctor, I made the statement that we expect that the right thing will be done in our presence or absent from us. That is so very important. Integrity requires that.

I knew a preacher once who said that there were two versions of him. He said there was the person people see on Sunday, and then there was the private, out of the public view person. I totally disagree with that assessment, and I believe that God does, too. Let us never forget that regardless of whether or not we are seen by people, God is omnipresent. He knows what we do all the time. Just knowing that is reason to want to maintain integrity. I tell members of my church that we should be the same people in the church as we are in the supermarket, at work, or anywhere else. Integrity is powerful. When we are reflecting Him, others will notice, and when they do, doors for witnessing can be opened that would be closed to those who demonstrate a lack of integrity. When we lack integrity, that is noticed too. The good news is that it can be changed!

I am not saying that we will never make any mistakes at all. Of course, we don't purposely set out to do wrong, but when we do falter, integrity is what makes us apologize to the person we offended. Integrity is what makes us admit that we were wrong. Integrity is what prevents us from lying even when telling the truth may cause us to be seen as weird or outcast. Integrity is the engine that spins the wheels of commitment. Your integrity should drive you to do what is right no matter what.

Integrity is the engine that spins the wheels of commitment.

Here is a story I read that beautifully illustrates what integrity should look like:

> Florida State University's sports information department had big news for Clay Shiver early this year [1995]: *Playboy* magazine had selected him for its preseason All-America football team. But quicker than he snaps the ball, the 6-foot-2, 280-pound center said, "No thanks."

"I couldn't see any good coming from being in the magazine," says Shiver, who has his eyes on the pros after graduation. "My mind was made up before it was offered to me."

The FSU business major adds: "It's almost funny how God works these things out even before we're faced with them." That's how it happened for Shiver.

Two weeks before he received the news, Shiver prayed about his response because the Seminoles' chaplain, Clint Purvis, was convinced he would be named to *Playboy's* team. Purvis asked Shiver what he would do. "I trust Clint a lot," says Shiver, who leads opening prayer and Scripture readings at First Baptist of Tallahassee's college worship services. "He knew I was going to be selected. It was like the Lord spoke to him."

Although the talented player realized this "honor" is one of the highest preseason awards a college football player can receive from sportswriters, it also meant an endorsement of *Playboy*. Clay didn't want to embarrass his mother and grandmother by appearing in the magazine or give old high school friends an excuse to buy that issue.

"Clay really gave up being named 'the best player in the country' at his position. It was a witness to people in the football program who wouldn't have known about Clay's faith," says Purvis, minister to students at First Baptist. "One Christian teammate said, 'I don't know if I could have turned it down.'"

But Shiver, an on-field leader with spiritual insight, cites Luke 12:48, "To whom much is given, much is required."

"I don't want to let anyone down, and number one on that list is God."[8]

God has given us a great privilege to be called His children. Having integrity should be treasured. Lives will be impacted by our integrity and I am sure that in the story you just read, Clay impacted lives for Christ by his stand for what was right. Having integrity means that we should do the same thing no matter what.

Chapter Seven Review

1. When you read the Clay Shiver story, what was your response?

   _____

   _____

2. True or false: Integrity means doing right when in the presence of others.

_____

_____

3. True or false: We should hate sin.

_____

_____

4. True or false: A person of integrity will never make mistakes.

_____

_____

5. True or false: A person of integrity will take some time to sin a little every now and then (gossip, lie, be critical, etc.).

_____

_____

6. Why do we need integrity?

_____

_____

_____

7. Do you have integrity? List ways you have exhibited integrity.

_____

_____

_____

_____

Endnotes

1. *The American Heritage College Dictionary,* 3rd ed., s.v. "integrity."

2. *Collins English Dictionary Complete & Unabridged,* 10th ed., s.v. "steadfast."

3. *Merriam-Webster Online,* s.v. "immovable," http://www.merriam-webster.com/dictionary/immovable (accessed January 28, 2011).

4. *Dictionary.com,* Dictionary.com Unabridged, Random House, Inc., s.v., "immovable," http://dictionary.reference.com/browse/immovable (accessed: January 28, 2011).

5. *Dictionary.com,* Dictionary.com Unabridged. Random House, Inc., s.v. "abounding," http://dictionary.reference.com/browse/abounding (accessed: January 28, 2011).

6. *The American Heritage College Dictionary,* 3rd ed., s.v. "integrity."

7. Dictionary.com, Dictionary.com Unabridged. Random House, Inc., s.v. "practice," http://dictionary.reference.com/browse/practice (accessed: January 28, 2011).

8. Rick White, "Growing Up in Our Commitment to Sexual Purity (9 of 12)," SermonSearch.com, http://www.sermonsearch.com/content.aspx?id=13960 (accessed January 29, 2011).

Chapter Eight

Essential Six:
Pray Always

The Bible tells us in Luke 18:1:

> *Now He was telling them a parable to show that at all times they ought to pray and not to lose heart...*

Prayer is our open line of communication with God. Disciples understand that prayer is not something that you only do when you feel bad or a crisis is imminent; prayer is a way of life! First Thessalonians 5:17 says, *"Pray without ceasing...."*

Prayer is our open line of communication with God.

What does it mean "always to pray" or to "pray without ceasing"? It certainly doesn't mean that we should constantly be repeating ritualistic prayers, because Jesus warned against that kind of praying.

> *When you pray, you are not to be like the hypocrites; for they love to stand and pray in the synagogues and on the street corners so that they may be seen by men. Truly I say to you, they have their reward in full. But you, when you pray, go into your inner room, close your door and pray to your Father who is in secret, and your Father who sees what is done in secret will reward you. And when you are praying, do not use meaningless repetition as the Gentiles do, for they suppose that they will be heard for their many words* (Matthew 6:5-7).

To pray without ceasing means to make prayer as natural to us as our regular breathing. We rarely think about our breathing; we just do it. Likewise with prayer—it should be the natural habit of our lives, the "atmosphere" in which we constantly live.

I find it interesting that in our country so much effort was put toward getting prayer out of schools and so much hostility is shown toward anything Christian. However, whenever America has encountered a crisis of some sort, what are we all encouraged to do? We are asked to pray for God to help! Prayer is important, and as Christians, we know that we should be praying daily, not only when a crisis comes.

We should desire to be effective in our prayer life. I believe that many people have a desire to know how to pray but neglect that aspect of their Christian life because they just don't know what to say. Jesus gave us a model prayer in His Sermon on the Mount. He said:

Pray, then, in this way: "Our Father, who is in heaven, hallowed be Your name. Your kingdom come. Your will be done, on earth as it is in heaven. Give us this day our daily bread. And forgive us our debts, as we also have forgiven our debtors. And do not lead us into temptation, but deliver us from evil. [For Yours is the kingdom and the power and the glory forever. Amen]" (Matthew 6:9-13).

This does not mean that all your prayers must say these exact words, but this is the model Jesus gave us. There are many good, solid, Bible-based books out on the subject of prayer, and I encourage you to get with your pastor and let him or her make a recommendation to you. My purpose here is not to give an exhaustive dissertation on the subject, but simply to highlight the fact that prayer is necessary and is to be a part of a disciple's life. It is in prayer that we communicate with God and get to know Him. It is in prayer that we hear from God and receive His direction. It is also in prayer that we bring our requests to God. Philippians 4:6-7 tells us:

Be anxious for nothing, but in everything by prayer and supplication with thanksgiving let your requests be made known to God. And the peace of God, which surpasses all comprehension, will guard your hearts and your minds in Christ Jesus.

So as you can see from this passage, prayer is an important stabilizer for our lives. God never intended for us to live separate from Him. He wants to have an intimate relationship with us. He wants to steer our lives, and this is achieved through an active prayer life. When we pray, we will know what God wants us to do, when He wants us to do it, how He wants us to do it, etc. He will guide us as we surrender to Him and seek to do His will. The churches in our world need to return to the biblical mandate to pray.

God never intended for us to live separate from Him.

Perhaps you would say, "Well, I thought that if I read my Bible, that was enough." Reading your Bible is certainly important; however, prayer is what takes you deeper into knowing how to apply God's Word to your life and live under the influence of His Spirit. If we are to live a life pleasing to God at all times, then we need to pray always.

Consider this. If you are reading this book and you are married, you will understand what I am about to say.

If you are not married, you will benefit from this truth if it is God's will that you will one day marry. In order for you to please your husband or wife, what is a key element in achieving that? The answer is easy. There must be *communication* in the relationship. Communication reveals what food your spouse likes best, what style clothing he or she likes, what his or her dreams and goals are, what he or she finds attractive in you, and the list can go on and on. Likewise, in our relationship with God, we must communicate to find out what God would have us to do for His glory.

Prayer is that open line of communication with God. Prayer is an important, necessary, and vital part of our lives. When I think of an example of a life of prayer, one person who stands out is the prophet Daniel. Daniel knew the importance of prayer. Daniel knew the necessity of prayer. Daniel knew how vital prayer was to his life. When faced with adversity, Daniel prayed. When things were fine, Daniel prayed. No matter how he felt, or what he faced, he prayed. Daniel's life is an example of the power of a consistent prayer life. Daniel was what many today may have considered a person who was "prayed up." What does that mean? Simply that his prayer life was so consistent that he was prepared for any obstacle and any test. His prayer life was so consistent that he didn't have to fret about whether God was going to come through; he knew that He would. What about you?

The key to Daniel's success was that he was consistent in his walk with God. Things that were intended by man to destroy him had no effect at all! The same applies to us. If we are consistent in our faith, we will find that whatever the devil meant for evil, God works it out for our good! This nearly 90-year-old man already had strong faith when he was faced with the punishment of being thrown in the lions' den in Daniel 6. How much stronger do you think his faith was to know that even the lions' den was no match for God?

The devil has thrown some things at some of you already that were intended to destroy you, but God protected you in the lions' den so that nothing harmed you. I know my family and I can testify about that in our own lives. This whole story of the lions' den is a monument to the keeping power of God.

The key to Daniel's success was that he was consistent in his walk with God.

Daniel's haters didn't intend on having the king sign a permanent injunction. They were just trying to get rid of Daniel. They knew he prayed three times a day, so it would be easy to catch him. They knew that once the king signed the injunction against such worship, he could not go back on his word. The devil will try some things to purposely cause you to get off track, abandon your faith, or even turn away from God. Daniel kept on doing business as usual, and so should we! His faith was consistent, and his victory was certain to manifest! Daniel was well liked by the king, but there were some in the kingdom who had their own agenda, and the only way they could implement their plan was to come up with a scheme to get Daniel out of the way.

First of all, they lied to get what they wanted. Let's put ourselves in Daniel's shoes here. These men told the king that all the leaders came together to decide on this proposal. Daniel was a high-ranking official in the kingdom, and he knew that he was not included in the meeting to decide on the injunction, although he should have been. The Lord showed me an acronym of the word L.I.O.N.S., and it so aptly describes this whole group of men. These men were Lying In Order To Negate Daniel's Service. Have you ever encountered any L.I.O.N.S. in your life? They knew Daniel wasn't included in the decision to go before the king to propose this injunction. However, Daniel's response was a sign of a man of prayer. What did he do?

1. After he knew the injunction had been signed, he did not go to the king to let him know how he felt about the matter. What would you have done? Would you have gone to give the king and all the schemers a piece of your mind?

2. After he knew the injunction had been signed and put into effect, he continued praying and praising God three times a day.

3. After the injunction had been signed, Daniel was aware of the risk involved by continuing his daily routine, but the risk was not worth abandoning his faith.

As I read this story, I wondered what Daniel prayed in Daniel 6:10. It's interesting that the Scripture specifies that it was *after* Daniel *"knew that the document was signed"* that he prayed. Of course, we can't say with any certainty what his exact words were, but the fact is that he prayed in the midst of adversity. I believe that part of his prayer dealt with the situation involving this 30-day injunction meant to keep him from praying to God. Daniel knew it wasn't right, so I believe he took that situation to God in prayer. He knew he wasn't going to stop praying upstairs in his room with the windows open; therefore, he was certain that he would probably visit the lions' den. I believe that he prayed and thanked God in advance for how He was going to move in this situation. Daniel did what we ought to do. Sometimes you can identify when the devil is just trying to show out. Rather than worry, or lose focus, take that situation to the Lord in prayer!

What was the motive behind these men drafting this proposal to present to the king?

1. They were jealous of Daniel. Daniel 6:3-4 tells us:

Then this Daniel began distinguishing himself among the commissioners and satraps because he possessed an extraordinary spirit, and the king planned to appoint him over the entire kingdom. Then the commissioners and satraps began trying to find a ground of accusation against Daniel in regard to government affairs; but they could find no ground of accusation or evidence of corruption, inasmuch as he was faithful, and no negligence or corruption was to be found in him.

2. Since they couldn't find anything he was doing wrong, they schemed a way to cause his devotion to God to work against him.

3. They had their own agenda, but they had to get Daniel out of the way first.

4. They were motivated to use this scheme because there was nothing else they could do!

Daniel didn't stop praying, and it wasn't long before these men were standing before the king to report that Daniel was not obeying the decree! (See Daniel 6:12-13.) They thought they got Daniel this time! They lied to get what they wanted, but the whole plan backfired because all of them and their families were devoured in the lions' den! (See Daniel 6:24.)

**Prayer does not guarantee you will exempt
yourself from adversity.**

Daniel was doing nothing wrong. God had blessed him for many years, but the haters were busy again! You might say, "Daniel prayed but still had to encounter the lions' den? Why?" My answer to you is that prayer does not guarantee you will exempt yourself from adversity. Your faith will be tested. However, what God doesn't take away from you, He makes a way for you to take! What these haters didn't know is that they weren't messing with a wimp in Daniel. An injunction wasn't going to stop him from getting on his knees to pray to God.

I believe that even in the lions' den, Daniel kept on praying.

Look at what happened:

1. He was untouched in the lions' den. God sent an angel to shut the lions' mouths (see Dan. 6:22). Not only were the lions tamed but so were the liars. They couldn't say anything now!

2. His enemies and their families were destroyed in the lions' den that they thought would be Daniel's death chamber (see Dan. 6:24).

3. The king came to know God himself.

4. The king gave a new order exalting the God of Daniel (see Dan. 6:26-27).

Consistent prayer is needed for us to have the kind of faith that can tame whatever lions we face in life.

> That kind of prayer life reminds me of a story about a small fortress deep in the Arabian Desert. Thomas Edward Lawrence, known as Lawrence of Arabia, often used it. It was modest but most sufficient. Its primary commendation was its security. When under attack, often by superior forces, Lawrence could retreat there. Then the resources of the fortress became his. The food and water stored there were life supporting. The strength of the fortification became the strength of its occupants. When Lawrence defended it, it defended him. As one relying on the garrison, he was the object of its protection. Its strength was his. Old desert dwellers living around there said that Sir Lawrence felt secure within its walls. He had on occasion to depend on the fort; it provided his need. He learned to trust it; his experience proved its worth. Like that fort, "the Lord is good, a stronghold in the day of trouble; and he knows them that trust in Him." Through prayer, we enter God's fortress.[1]

The devil goes about as a roaring lion seeking whom he may devour. There's no need to worry, because all he's doing is making a whole lot of noise! There's nothing like a praying child of God!

Chapter Eight Review

1. What were Daniel's haters trying to do to him?

_____

_____

_____

2. What happened when Daniel prayed about his situation?

_____

_____

_____

3. What does it mean to pray without ceasing?

_____

_____

_____

_____

4. Where do we find the model for prayer that Jesus gave His disciples?

_____

_____

5. According to Philippians 4:6-7, what happens after we make our requests known to God?

_____

_____

_____

6. Prayer is an open line of communication to God. Why is it necessary to use this open line of communication?

_____

_____

_____

Endnote

1. James S. Hewitt, *Illustrations Unlimited* (Wheaton, IL, Tyndale House Publishers).

Essential Seven: Loving Others Is the Mark of a True Disciple

If we say we are Christians, and we do not show love to others, we are lacking an understanding of what a true disciple is. John 13:34-35 says:

> *A new commandment I give to you, that you love one another, even as I have loved you, that you also love one another. By this all men will know that you are My disciples, if you have love for one another.*

When first reading this Scripture, you would be led to believe that loving one another is a new commandment. To love one another was not a new commandment. Leviticus 19:18 says:

> *You shall not take vengeance, nor bear any grudge against the sons of your people, but you shall love your neighbor as yourself; I am the lord.*

The difference is that in John, instead of loving one another as yourself, Jesus says love one another even as I have loved you! Jesus loved us sacrificially! The love being commanded is the love of Jesus Himself, which is the love of God Himself, the love that can be shed abroad in our hearts only by the Holy Spirit.

And hope does not disappoint, because the love of God has been poured out within our hearts through the Holy Spirit who was given to us (Romans 5:5).

Only the Spirit of God can put the love of Jesus within the heart of the believer. The Holy Spirit can create within the believer the love of Jesus Himself, the very same love Jesus had while here on Earth.

Only the Spirit of God can put the love of Jesus within the heart of the believer.

Here are a few questions you should ask yourself. Do you love people? Do people know you love them? What have you done to show your love? Do you love the way Christ did? Many people have many misconceptions about the Church. People think the Church is a bunch of self-centered, self-righteous fanatics. Some think the Church is a scam. Some believe that all the Church is after is money. Unfortunately, there have been enough instances of misconduct in the Church plastered all over the local and national news that a person can find it difficult to put trust in an institution that preaches a message it does not live. Of course, there are many great, strong, Bible-based churches that exist in our world, but when was the last time you heard about them on the news?

There needs to be a paradigm shift in the way the Church thinks of itself, which in turn will result in a change in the way the world around us thinks of the Church. What do I mean? Simply put, people in the Church need to get out of the business of identifying everyone's faults and shortcomings. The Word of God and the Spirit of God will do whatever convicting, reproving, and rebuking needs to be done. The Church needs to proclaim what everyone needs to hear: the Word of God. Ironically, in our culture of trying to appease and appeal to everyone, I believe that people really want to hear the truth of God's Word and not something that is so watered down as to have no power. Here is the formula for change: *Get back to the business of loving people!* If we really love people we will preach the Word of God *because* we love them.

Here is a something that may come as a shock to some who will read this book: The Church is not about any one man or woman! The Church is all about Jesus! Jesus loved others and we are commanded to do so as well. He gave the greatest demonstration of love ever when He endured what He did on the cross for us.

Hebrews 12:2 gives us a glimpse of how much He loved us:

Fixing our eyes on Jesus, the author and perfecter of faith, who for the joy set before Him endured the cross, despising the shame, and has sat down at the right hand of the throne of God.

Did you see that? It said that He endured the cross because of the joy set before Him! What was that joy? It was the payment of the penalty of sin so that we could be free! If you haven't accepted Christ as your Savior, or if you haven't shared the good news with someone else, why haven't you?

Love is the hallmark of a disciple of Christ.

Love is the hallmark of a disciple of Christ. In John 13:34-35, Jesus said:

A new commandment I give to you, that you love one another, even as I have loved you, that you also love one another. By this all men will know that you are My disciples, if you have love for one another.

We must love others. Here are a few reasons why:

1. *We love others because* as Christians, we follow someone who met the needs of others, no matter what. In Matthew 22:36-37, 39, He was asked the

question, *"Which is the great commandment in the Law?"* His answer was twofold. First, He said we are to love the Lord our God with all our heart, soul, and mind. Second, He said to love your neighbor as yourself. The key ingredient in that twofold answer is *love*. This someone who commanded that we do these things is Jesus Christ.

2. *We love others because* Jesus didn't just say to love God and love your neighbor and that's it. He gave us the greatest example of love ever given when He endured the cross for us to pay the penalty for our sin so that we could be free. He went out of His way to do something He really was not obligated to do so that we would benefit. The love God has for us is real. In the December 4, 1989, issue of *Newsweek* magazine, there was an article about a little-known mental disorder called erotomania. It is a mental illness in which a person has the delusion that he or she is the object of someone's love. Some imagine love affairs that continue for years, yet it all exists only in the imagination of the sufferer. The title of the article was "The Delusions of Love." While romantic love may have many delusions, there is no delusion about God's love.[1]

3. *We love others because* that same love that God has for us is *in* us! That love, according to Romans 5:5, has been poured out within our own hearts

through the Holy Spirit, who was given to us. Jesus gave us many examples of what love should look like, and it is our endeavor to demonstrate that same love.

4. *We love others because* the love that God, through His son, Jesus Christ, showed toward us, and placed in us by the Holy Spirit, must be put into action. Consider the following illustration:

> One day, a man was trying to read a serious book, but his little boy kept interrupting him. He would lean against his knees and say, "Daddy, I love you." The father would give him a pat and say rather absently, "Yes, Son, I love you too," and he would kind of give him a little push away so he could keep on reading. But this didn't satisfy the boy, and finally he ran to his father and said, "I love you, Daddy," and he jumped up on his lap and threw his arms around him and gave him a big squeeze, explaining, "And I've just got to do something about it!" That's it—as we grow in love, we aren't content with small-talk love, or pat on the head love. We want to get involved and "do something about it."[2]

5. *We love others because* of the opportunity to make a difference. The Bible tells us in Galatians 6:10:

"So then, while we have opportunity, let us do good to all people, and especially to those who are of the household of the faith [or the family of believers]." Opportunities to make a difference are all around us. Whether it's a smile that brightens someone's day, a kind word to lift someone's spirit, a helping hand to accomplish a much-needed task, a random act of kindness, a word of prayer to give hope in a time of need, or a listening ear to someone needing someone to listen—the list could go on and on. Jesus shared a very important principle in the latter half of Matthew 10:8 when He said, *"Freely you have received, freely give."* Because we have freely received the love of God, we likewise should freely share it to impact lives to the glory of God. If we say we are Christians that means we should be Christlike. He loves us unconditionally. We should love the same way, otherwise we are nothing. The following illustration beautifully depicts what our love should look like. It says:

> If we have diplomas and degrees and know all the up-to-date methods, and have not His touch of understanding love, we are nothing. If we are able to argue successfully against the religions of the people and make fools of them, and have not His wooing note, we are nothing. If we have all faith and great ideals and magnificent plans, and

not His love that sweats and bleeds and weeps and prays and pleads, we are nothing. If we give our clothes and money to others, and have not His love for others, we are nothing. If we surrender all prospects, leave home and friends, make the sacrifices of a missionary career, and turn sour and selfish amid the daily annoyances and slights of a missionary life, and have not the love that yields its rights, its leisures, its pet plans, we are nothing. Virtue has ceased to go out of us. If we can heal all manner of sickness and disease, but wound hearts and hurt feelings for want of His love that is kind, we are nothing. If we can write articles or publish books that win applause, but fail to transcribe the Word of the Cross into the language of His love, we are nothing.— South African Pioneer[3]

The distinguishing mark of a true believer is not the normal human love of neighbors, not even the love of brothers and sisters or of husband and wife. It is the spiritual and supernatural love of Jesus Himself that dwells within the life of the believer.

This kind of love attracts unbelievers to Christ. By this love shall all men know that a person is a *true* disciple of the Lord.

Chapter Nine Review

1. Why should we love others?

_____

_____

_____

2. How did Christ show His love toward us?

_____

_____

_____

3. What is the mark of a true disciple?

_____

_____

_____

4. What is the Scripture that explains how others will know that we are Christ's disciples?

_____

_____

_____

5. What were the five reasons given for why we should love?

_____

_____

_____

_____

6. Can you think of ways you've shown God's love to someone in the past week or month? List those ways here.

_____

_____

_____

_____

7. What can we do to help change the mindsets of people in the world about church?

_____

_____

_____

_____

_____

Endnotes

1. Robert C. Shannon, *1000 Windows* (Cincinnati, OH: Standard Publishing Company, 1997).

2. James S. Hewitt, *Illustrations Unlimited* (Wheaton, IL: Tyndale House Publishers), 329.

3. Pastor's Library Software, Logos Bible Software version of P. L. Tan, *Encyclopedia of 7,700 Illustrations* (Garland TX: Bible Communications, 1996).

Essential Eight: Enduring Until the End

God never promised us that this life would be easy. He never promised us that everything would go our way all the time. He never promised us that we would never go through hard times in life.

Suffer hardship with me, as a good soldier of Christ Jesus (2 Timothy 2:3).

If we endure, we will also reign with Him; if we deny Him, He also will deny us; (2 Timothy 2:12).

And we know that God causes all things to work together for good to those who love God, to those who are called according to His purpose (Romans 8:28).

When we keep this in mind, we will continue to see that God knows best, and He never makes a mistake.

Therefore be patient, brethren, until the coming of the Lord. See how the farmer waits for the precious fruit of the earth, waiting patiently for it until it receives the early and latter rain. You also be patient. Establish your hearts, for the coming of the Lord is at hand. Do not grumble against one another, brethren, lest you be condemned. Behold, the Judge is standing at the door! My brethren, take the prophets, who spoke in the name of the Lord, as an example of suffering and patience. Indeed we count them blessed who endure. You have heard of the perseverance of Job and seen the end intended by the Lord—that the Lord is very compassionate and merciful (James 5:7-11 NKJV).

When you see the word *therefore,* you have to look at verses preceding it to see what the word is there for. The same applies to any literature. There are certain words in our English language that mandate that we either gather a proper understanding of the prior text or gain some other clarification of why the word is there. In this case, I believe the word marks a digression or change of focus from those who were misusing riches and getting richer by means of sinful practices to those who were perhaps victimized by these evil men. James' message here is one of patience and perseverance. His words help strengthen them, as well as us today, that no matter what, we have to be patient to wait and persevere in service to the Lord— and to do it knowing that His coming is at hand, and we will receive our precious reward. James uses three examples to illustrate his point.

> No matter what, we have to be patient to wait and persevere in service to the Lord...

The Farmer

There are several observations when you break down the example of the farmer given in James 5. The farmer cannot be someone who is always in a hurry, but he must learn to have patience while he waits, and he must have perseverance to carry on the work. Now this is what the Holy Spirit revealed to me when I was preparing the outline of this passage.

Before anything can happen, the farmer has to plant the seeds. Although it does not say the farmer planted, it is an obvious deduction that he must have planted in order to see anything come forth.

After he plants, he must wait, but we cannot miss a key part of this passage, which is the timing of his planting. The farmer has to know his stuff! The passage speaks of the early and the latter rain. He has to know when the early rain comes, and he has to plant his seed before it comes. This is a vital piece of information he needs to know, because once the seed is planted, it must be watered. It cannot just stay in the ground for long periods of time with no water, because it will die. In Israel, the early rain comes in October and November just after the seed is sown. The latter rain comes in March and April, just before the harvest comes.

The early rain helps prepare the seed to manifest a harvest. The early rain helps that seed anchor some roots in the ground, because before the seed can grow up, it must grow down. However, it still needs more rain.

While the farmer is waiting, he doesn't just stand around with his hands in his pockets like he has nothing to do; he has to care for that ground. He can't just plant seed and say, "OK, Lord, the rest is up to You now! I'm tired! I'm going to have a seat now, Lord, by the juniper tree and take a nap. Come on now, Lord, and bless us." The farmer has to keep working to ensure that his harvest is plentiful. He has weeds to pull, because if he doesn't, the weeds will choke out the seed's potential, and there will be no harvest. He has to guard the ground against intruders, to ensure that what has been planted is not adversely affected.

While he is doing all of this, the seed begins to produce evidence of growth. He doesn't stop there, but he keeps on waiting and persevering. Then the latter rain comes and helps the precious fruit come to fruition.

What we can gather from this first example of James is that we are all waiting for the coming of the Lord. There was a time we had no concern about the things of God, but thanks be to God, one day, a seed was planted. That seed was the Word of God! After that seed was planted, it had to be watered by the early rain of Bible study, prayer, and faithful church attendance. And after it took root in us, and there was evidence of growth, the latter rain of Bible study, prayer, and faithful church attendance helped to bring forth fruit in us and prepare us to be a sanctified vessel fit to be used by God. The ground that the seed was planted in was our heart. It reminds me of the parable of the four soils Jesus gave, which is recorded in Matthew, Mark, and Luke. I saw a wonderful description of the four soils from Bible.org:

> *The hardened soil*—those along the path—are those whose hearts have never been open to the gospel, who never responded positively to the Lord Jesus Christ. The scribes and Pharisees seem generally to fall into this category. The gospel makes no impression on them whatsoever. Satan immediate snatches the gospel from their hearts, so that there is no response, no new birth, and no fruit.
>
> *The second soil—the shallow soil—* represents those who positively (joyfully) respond to our Lord's teaching, but only due to an inadequate grasp of

its implications. These folks respond positively to the Word because they think that it is a kind of "prosperity gospel," a gospel which promises only good times, blessing, happiness, and bliss. The quickness of the response is an indication of their lack of depth, or their lack of perception as to what the gospel really means. And, let me quickly add, this is not due to our Lord's misrepresentation of the gospel. It is the result of selective hearing, of hearing only the good and pleasant things, rather than hearing of the costs involved in discipleship, of which our Lord often spoke. A simple reading of the Sermon on the Mount will show how our Lord carefully represented the blessings and the costs of following Him.

The third soil, the thorny soil, represents those who have a more complete grasp of the cost of discipleship, but who have never rid themselves of the "cares of this world." Their concerns for money and for pleasure outgrow their seeking first the Kingdom of God, and thus their priorities are reversed. It is not that the people represented by this thorny soil do not understand the costs of discipleship, but that they are not willing to pay the price.

It is not lack of knowledge which causes them to err, but lack of commitment, lack of dedication.

The fourth soil, the good soil represents all those whose hearts are prepared for the gospel, and whose lives are uncluttered with competitive interests and values. In this fourth soil the Word not only brings forth life, but the plant comes to maturity and it bears fruit. Here is the goal of discipleship.[1]

We've got to persevere while we wait, knowing that the precious coming of the Lord is nigh!

Which one describes you? Like the farmer, we've got to keep the soil free of clutter. We've got to guard the soil from attack of the enemy. We've got to pull out the weeds of sin that can choke out the fruit God is trying to produce in us, and we've got to persevere while we wait, knowing that the precious coming of the Lord is nigh!

James told them:

1. Be patient.

2. Establish your hearts.

3. Do not grumble (grumbling can cause discouragement).

4. Act like the Lord is standing at the door and coming at any moment!

James used the example of the prophets too, and this example James used ought to encourage us:

1. To stay committed to God

2. To endure the hardness of this life, knowing that our reward is on the other side. *"For everything that was written in the past was written to teach us, so that through endurance and the encouragement of the Scriptures we might have hope"* (Rom. 15:4 NIV).

3. To know that God has provided the way to endure by His Spirit, by His Word, and by His Church

Then James used the example of Job, mentioning him in James 5:11. The Book of Job describes this man as "blameless," and "upright":

There was a man in the land of Uz whose name was Job; and that man was blameless, upright fearing God and turning away from evil. Seven sons and three daughters were born to him. His possessions also were 7,000 sheep, 3,000 camels, 500 yoke of oxen, 500 female donkeys, and very many servants; and that man was the greatest of all the men of the east (Job 1:1-3).

Job was a righteous man. Job was a blessed man. Job was a man who feared God. Job was a man who seemingly had never gone through anything difficult until now. Job was unaware of what was going on behind the scenes. Everything was all right in Job's world, but suddenly things changed. He lost everything he had.

It seemed like everything was against him. His wife was against him, for she told him, *"Curse God and die"* (Job 2:9). His friends were against him, for they accused him of being a hypocrite, deserving of the judgment of God. And it seemed like God was against him! When Job cried out for answers to his questions, there was no reply from Heaven.

Job endured. Satan predicted that Job would get impatient with God and abandon his faith, but that did not happen. It is true that Job questioned God's will, but Job did not forsake his faith in the Lord. In Job 13:15, Job said:

Though He slay me, I will hope in Him. Nevertheless
I will argue my ways before Him.

Job patiently endured. He said:

He knows the way I take; when He has tried me, I
shall come forth as gold (Job 23:10).

He will not be just any gold, but gold that has some greater value. Some of you may be going through the fire right now in your lives. You may not understand why you are in the trial you are in, but God has a plan. God has His hand on the thermostat, and when the trial is over, you shall be like gold! The lesson James wanted them to know, and what the Word is saying to us through Job's example, is that there is a greater blessing after the trial!

Satan wants us to get impatient with God, for an impatient Christian is a powerful weapon in the devil's hands. We must be patient. Patience is not something we do; it is something we are. Moses' lack of patience robbed him of a trip to the Holy Land; Abraham's lack of patience led to the birth of Ishmael, the enemy of the Jews; and Peter's lack of patience almost made him a murderer. When satan attacks us, it is easy for us to get impatient and run ahead of God and lose God's blessing as a result. It is also easy for us to simply give up and quit altogether, but we have to be soldiers and endure. Failure to be patient can rob us of a blessing that may be about to unfold tomorrow! Jesus is coming! We don't know the hour, but we have to live our lives faithfully and wait patiently, knowing that what the Lord has said, He will do.

**Patience is not something we do;
it is something we are.**

James has shown us that there is a blessing in waiting patiently, knowing that the coming of the Lord is nigh. You may have already been waiting a long time. You might think the Lord has forgotten all about your situation; just know that He who has begun a good work in you is able to perform it until the day of Jesus Christ (see Phil. 1:6). You might say, "Pastor, I don't feel like a good work is being done in me. I've been going through this a long time." I want you to know that although your night may have been long, trouble doesn't last always. "Well, Pastor, I've been walking a long time. How long do I have to wait?" I can't answer the question of how long, but I can promise you:

> *They that wait upon the lord shall renew their strength; they shall mount up with wings as eagles; they shall run, and not be weary; and they shall walk, and not faint* (Isaiah 40:31 KJV).

"Well, Pastor, I hear that, but I've been waiting a long time!" I say to you, my brothers and sisters: "Keep on waiting."

My mind goes to the fact that Jesus Himself waited patiently. He waited patiently for the time when He should leave the sacred halls of Heaven and take His place in the form of a babe planted in the womb of a virgin. John 1:1 says: *"In the beginning was the Word, and the Word was with God, and the Word was God."* He said a few verses later, *"The Word became flesh, and dwelt among us..."* (John 1:14). But before He could come forth, He had to wait. For nine months, the precious baby Jesus dwelt in the womb of Mary until the time that He should come forth and grace the world with His presence. He waited patiently, for He knew that the time would come for His purpose to be fulfilled on this earth. He waited. He waited for 33 years until the time of His death was nigh. He waited. He waited until the first day of that holy week that we recognize as Palm Sunday, to enter in to that Holy City Jerusalem, in fulfillment of the prophecy of Zechariah 9:9-10, which said:

> *Rejoice greatly, O daughter of Zion! Shout in triumph, O daughter of Jerusalem! Behold, your king is coming to you; He is just and endowed with salvation, humble, and mounted on a donkey, even on a colt, the foal of a donkey. I will cut off the chariot from Ephraim and the horse from Jerusalem; and the bow of war will be cut off. And He will speak peace to the nations; and His dominion will be from sea to sea, and from the River to the ends of the earth.*

As he entered the city, they laid down their garments to cushion His ride, and they laid down palm fronds in front of Him as a symbol of triumph. Yes, He waited. While evil men tried the Lord of glory and found no fault, He waited. He could have ended it at any time since He was God in the flesh, but He waited. While wicked men beat Him and mocked Him and scorned Him, He waited. As He hung on the cross, He waited. He waited and endured the cross because of the joy that was set before Him, which was the redemption of man. He waited. He could have called tens of thousands of angels to carry Him away, but He waited until He could utter the words,

"It is finished." While He was in the tomb, all the host of Heaven waited for the third day when He would rise again, and He did! But the waiting wasn't over, for He waited for 40 more days before He left this earth and ascended into Heaven. As He was ascending, the angels gave us a promise when they said:

> ...*Why stand ye gazing up into heaven? This same Jesus, which is taken up from you into heaven, shall so come in like manner as ye have seen him go into heaven!* (Acts 1:11 KJV).

So now *we* wait. We wait patiently for the Lord to come receive us unto Himself and fulfill the words of First Corinthians 15:51-52, which says:

> *Behold, I shew you a mystery; we shall not all sleep, but we shall all be changed, in a moment, in the twinkling of an eye, at the last trump: for the trumpet shall sound, and the dead shall be raised incorruptible, and we shall be changed* (KJV).

But while we wait, we must keep on preaching. While we wait, we must keep on witnessing. While we wait, we've got to keep fasting. While we wait, we've got to keep on praying. While we wait, the hungry still need to be fed. While we wait, the hurting still need to know love. While we wait, the stranger still needs to be welcomed in. While we wait, the naked still need to be clothed. While we wait, the prisoner needs to know that there is hope.

While we wait, we've got to keep pressing on. While we wait, we've got to keep looking to Jesus, the author and finisher of our faith. While we wait, we've got to remember the words of the Lord when He said in John 14:1-3:

> *Let not your heart be troubled: ye believe in God, believe also in Me. In My Father's house are many mansions: if it were not so, I would have told you. I go to prepare a place for you. And if I go and prepare a place for you, I will come again, and receive you unto Myself; that where I am, there ye may be also* (KJV).

In the Christian world, many think that life is supposed to be trouble-free and prosperous. The Lord does desire for us to prosper and be in good health, but He also desires our souls to prosper (see 3 John 2). True prosperity is twofold: natural and spiritual. However, anything worth achieving requires some endurance to attain.

Anything worth achieving requires some endurance to attain.

When an athlete has a goal of being a champion, it takes endurance, discipline, and commitment. Paul understood the correlation between an athlete's endurance and that of the Christian life. Paul wrote in Hebrews 12:1-3:

> *Therefore, since we have so great a cloud of witnesses surrounding us, let us also lay aside every encumbrance*

and the sin which so easily entangles us, and let us run with endurance the race that is set before us, fixing our eyes on Jesus, the author and perfecter of faith, who for the joy set before Him endured the cross, despising the shame, and has sat down at the right hand of the throne of God. For consider Him who has endured such hostility by sinners against Himself, so that you will not grow weary and lose heart.

Endurance builds character. Life can be difficult, but we must endure.

Second Timothy 2:3 says:

Endure hardship with us like a good soldier of Christ Jesus (NIV).

Without endurance, we will never see God move on our behalf because we will always be quitters. It's like the athlete who desires to be great but quits after a few losses or setbacks. What kind of athlete would that be? Likewise, what kind of Christian would you be if you gave up whenever things got a little tough? We all will go through some tests and trials, but it's all a part of the process of becoming what God would have us to be (see 1 Pet. 4:12).

We have no basis for quitting if we truly believe the Scripture found at Philippians 4:13.

Jesus endured for us. Jesus suffered so much for our sake. He suffered so that we would not have to be doomed to die and be eternally separated from God because of our sins. He did it willingly. Hebrews 12:2 says:

Fixing our eyes on Jesus, the author and perfecter of faith, who for the joy set before Him endured the cross, despising the shame, and has sat down at the right hand of the throne of God.

Dr. C. Truman Davis gave a vivid description of what Jesus endured on the cross. He wrote:

The cross is placed on the ground and the exhausted man is quickly thrown backwards with his shoulders against the wood. The legionnaire feels for the depression at the front of the wrist. He drives a heavy, square wrought-iron nail through the wrist and deep into the wood. Quickly he moves to the other side and repeats the action, being careful not to pull the arms too tightly, but to allow some flex and movement. The cross is then lifted into place.

The left foot is pressed backward against the right foot, and with both feet extended, toes down, a nail is driven through the arch of each, leaving the knees flexed. The victim is now crucified. As he slowly sags down with more weight on the nails in the wrists, excruciating, fiery pain shoots along the fingers and up the arms to explode in the brain—the nails in the wrists are putting pressure on the median nerves. As he pushes himself upward to avoid this stretching torment, he places the full weight on the nail through his feet. Again he feels the searing agony of the nail tearing through the nerves between the bones of his feet. As the arms fatigue, cramps sweep through the muscles, knotting them in deep, relentless, throbbing pain. With these cramps comes the inability to push himself upward to breathe. Air can be drawn into the lungs but not exhaled. He fights to raise himself in order to get even one small breath. Finally carbon dioxide builds up in the lungs and in the blood stream, and the cramps partially subside. Spasmodically he is able to push himself upward to exhale and bring in life-giving oxygen.

Hours of this limitless pain, cycles of twisting, joint-rending cramps, intermittent partial asphyxiation, searing pain as tissue is torn from his lacerated back as he moves up and down against the rough timber. Then another agony begins: a deep, crushing pain deep in the chest as the pericardium slowly fills with serum and begins to compress the heart. It is now almost over—

the loss of tissue fluids has reached a critical level—the compressed heart is struggling to pump heavy, thick, sluggish blood into the tissues—the tortured lungs are making a frantic effort to gasp in small gulps of air. He can feel the chill of death creeping through his tissues . . . Finally he can allow his body to die.

All this the Bible records with the simple words, *"And they crucified Him"* (Mark 15:24).[2]

No greater love has any man than this! What we have to endure cannot even compare to what He endured, and we have Him to help us live the life He has prescribed for us to live.

Chapter 10 Review

1. What are two verses of Scripture that indicate that we will probably encounter some difficulty in life? What difficulty have you encountered? What did you learn from it?

_____

_____

_____

2. Even though we encounter difficulty, what verse
indicates that everything is working in our favor?

_____

_____

_____

3. Is it better to trust your own plan or God's? Why?

_____

_____

_____

_____

4. What are some key things you observed about the
farmer?

_____

_____

_____

5. How can you apply the lesson of the farmer to your
life?

_____

_____

_____

6. What can we learn from the example of the prophets that James uses?

_____

_____

_____

_____

7. What can we learn from Job's life?

_____

_____

_____

_____

8. Which soil best represents you?

_____

_____

9. While we wait on the coming of the Lord, what should we be doing?

_____

_____

_____

_____

10. What verse of Scripture indicates that we have no basis for quitting if we truly believe it?

_____

_____

11. Is there anything you can think of that remotely compares to what Christ endured for you?

_____

_____

_____

12. What does Hebrews 12:2 mean to you?

_____

_____

Endnotes

1. Bob Deffinbaugh, "Parable of the Soils (Luke 8:4-21)," *bible.org,* http://bible.org/seriespage/parable-soils-luke-84-21 (accessed January 28, 2011).

2. Adaptation of C. Truman Davis, M.D., *The Expositor's Bible Commentary, Vol. 8,* as quoted in "Crucifixion," *Sermon Illustrations.com,* http://www.sermonillustrations.com/a-z/c/crucifixion.htm (accessed January 28, 2011).

Always Trust in God

I pray that this book has caused you to take a serious, introspective look at yourself and that you have begun to see change in your life as you have applied the essentials. I know there will be times when you will want to throw in the towel and give up. There will be times of great euphoria, and everything in between these two feelings.

Don't pick and choose parts of God's Word, but rely on the full counsel of God.

In today's culture, people rely on a number of things. They rely on horoscopes, tarot card readings, karma, self-help books, luck, and I'm sure you can think of a number of other things to add to the list. However, as disciples, there is only one thing we should continually feed ourselves on, and that is the Word of God. Don't pick and choose parts of God's Word, but rely on the full counsel of God. It is the

Word of God that must be preached. It is the Word of God that we must obey. It is the Word of God that brings about real change. It is the Word of God through which we must filter every action, every relationship, every thought, and in fact, everything! No matter what may currently be going on in your life, always stay dependent on God's Word and you will be blessed. Obey His Word even when it does not seem to make any sense to you to do so. Remember what the Bible says in Isaiah 55:9:

> *For as the heavens are higher than the earth, so are My ways higher than your ways and My **thoughts** than your **thoughts.***

In other words, God knows what is best, no matter what. There is a story in the Book of Luke that illustrates this perfectly. Luke 5:1-7 says:

> *Now it happened that while the crowd was pressing around Him and listening to the word of God, He was standing by the lake of Gennesaret; and He saw two boats lying at the edge of the lake; but the fishermen had gotten out of them and were washing their nets. And He got into one of the boats, which was Simon's, and asked him to put out a little way from the land. And He sat down and **began** teaching the people from the boat. When He had finished speaking, He said to Simon, **"Put out into the deep water and let down your nets for a catch."** Simon answered and said, "Master, we*

*worked hard all night and caught nothing, but I will do as You say **and** let down the nets." When they had done this, they enclosed a great quantity of fish, and their nets **began** to break; so they signaled to their partners in the other boat for them to come and help them. And they came and filled both of the boats, so that they began to sink.*

As you read this story, it is obvious that the fishermen had given up. They struggled all night and caught nothing. Why did they fail? Surely it wasn't that they did not know how or where to fish. These men were experts. They were professional fishermen and knew how to fish and where to find the fish. Yet they fished all night long and caught nothing. Their failure had nothing to do with how they were fishing or where they were fishing. Their failure came about because the Lord wanted to teach them a much-needed lesson. That lesson is that without Him, we can accomplish nothing!

They were probably discouraged. They had tried all night long to bring in a catch, but they caught nothing in their nets.

A discouraged minister once dreamed that he was standing on the top of a great granite rock, trying to break it with a pickaxe. Hour after hour, he worked on with no result. At last he said, "It is useless; I will stop." Suddenly a man stood by him and asked, "Were you not allotted this task? And if so, why are you going to abandon it?" "My work is in vain; I can make no impression on the granite," was the minister's reply. Then the stranger solemnly replied, "That is nothing to you; your duty is to pick, whether the rock yields or no. The work is yours, the results are in other hands; work on." In his dream the minister saw himself setting out anew his labor, and at his first blow the rock flew into hundreds of pieces.[1]

We see that the men gave up but then Jesus spoke up. He told Peter to launch out into the deep for a catch. Even though they had caught nothing all night, Jesus told them to cast their nets again! I can just imagine the looks on their faces when Jesus said to go out and cast their nets again. One thing that you must remember here is that these guys were not just casual, recreational fishermen. These guys were professionals! Peter was probably thinking to himself, "Did Jesus hear what I said? I already told Him that we've been fishing all night and we caught nothing!" They were fine staying close to shore, but Jesus said, "Launch!"

They were fine staying close to shore, but Jesus said, "Launch!"

I'm sure Peter, like many of us, really didn't want to. I can imagine Simon Peter and his partners were ready to call it a day. They had fished all night long and had caught not so much as a single little fish. They were tired, frustrated, discouraged, and defeated. The last thing any of them wanted to do was go back out and fish some more. That sounds just like some of us Christians when we've tried something one time or a few times. We really don't want to keep trying. We hear the Word keep telling us to persevere. We keep hearing the Word telling us not to give up. We keep hearing the Word say not to quit, but that's really not what we want to hear. However, just as Jesus wanted to teach them a much-needed lesson, the same goes for us.

I remember a time when my family and I had to persevere. God had already revealed to me that He was calling us to start a church. In order to start the church we had to sell our home and move to another city. We had already started building our new home in the other city, when out of nowhere, I was laid off. The company I worked for was bought out! At that moment, I began to question whether or not this move was of God. How could we move now when I didn't have a job? How would we close on our house with no employment? Many other things went through my head, but God opened a door for another job. The new job wasn't paying nearly as much as the old one, but we were thankful. By the way, the house we had on the market did sell, and at the time I got the new job we were living in an extended stay hotel with our five small kids. Our time in the extended stay was three months! I thought about giving up on the vision of starting a church, but I am glad I did not. I am glad my wife persevered, too. It was a test of faith. Either God called us to this assignment and the church would be birthed, or we just didn't really hear God!

One night, we went to the house that was being built after we were told that there were other people looking at the house and interested in buying it since we no longer had the income we had before. We stood in that house and told God that we believed He was going to bring us out of that situation and we declared that the house would be used for ministry. Shortly afterward, we closed on the house with money God provided from an unexpected source!

There was another time when perseverance was needed. We had been displaced from our building because of a terrible fire that did major damage. We were displaced for almost six months while repairs were being done. During that time we had to use hotels, conference centers, etc., to hold our worship services. During this time when we all needed to stick together and support one another, people began to leave the ministry. I would get e-mails from people saying things such as, the ministry has changed so we have to go. I e-mailed a few people trying to ask why they were leaving and got no response.

The strangest thing to me was that people who were leaving were saying how much they loved us as they were leaving and prior to the fire these people all proclaimed how much they loved us and the church! None of them cited anything actually wrong with the church or any wrongdoing on the part of me or my wife. They just had a "feeling" that their "season" had ended. It made no sense. I could understand if we were mistreating people or not preaching the Word or perhaps showed no love and concern for the people. However, none of that was true.

All of this really hurt my wife and me. To add to the pain, these people who proclaimed to love us and the church said negative things about us to others behind our backs even before they left. Even though we received such unnecessary treatment, we never retaliated against any of them. There have been members of the church who have stated how blessed they were to see us stay the course and continue in the ministry in spite of how things looked. Others have said they observed how we dealt with people. We did it while enduring *much pain* inside. The weight of ministry got heavy. Quitting sounded like a great idea. Church and personal finances had diminished, and stress was mounting. In the midst of it all, we had to keep pressing forward. We did it because of all the dedicated people who did stay with us. We did it because of the changed lives that had been impacted by our ministry. We did it because God called us to this assignment and we could not abandon the people who really did love us, the way other people had abandoned us. We hold no animosity toward the departed. To this day, if they were in need of any help, we would help them because of the love of God in our hearts.

I believe God is trying to see how determined we are to get the blessing He has promised, and He wants us to totally surrender ourselves to Him.

Peter did something that totally went against his own sense of reason because of the Word of the Lord. That's a lesson we all need to learn and really internalize. When Jesus told Peter to launch into the deep, Peter surrendered to the will of the Lord and went out to fish. There are times when the Lord asks us to do certain things that we may not want to do and may not make sense to us. However, we must come to the same place Peter came. We need to decide that regardless of how we feel about a certain matter, if the Lord has commanded it, then we will cast our nets even if we've already tried before! Some people say, "If your heart isn't in it, then you might as well not do it!" That is wrong thinking! God will reward our obedience if we will go ahead and do what He has told us to do. When we obey in spite of our own objections, the heart will eventually follow our lead.

These men gave up, Jesus spoke up, and then their nets filled up! The blessing was more than they could handle. One thing I want you to see here is that it was not the next day or the next night when their nets filled up, but it was *immediately!* I want you to know that even though you may have pressed your way all year long and it may seem like you can't press on any more, your day of breakthrough is coming. When you think you've done all you can, cast your net again and watch God change things for you suddenly!

This shows me that the Lord's word is sure. Jesus didn't tell them to cast their nets and see *if* they could catch something. He told them to cast their nets *for* a catch! Psalm 145:13 says, *"...The lord is faithful to all His promises and loving toward all He has made"* (NIV).

This also shows me that it's not over until God says it's over! Maybe you've been struggling all year or for many years trying to accomplish goals you set, and now it seems like the night is over and you've given up. Even when you get discouraged, you've got to keep casting your net! It's time for some of us to get out of the comfort zone close to the shore and launch out in the deep! Just like Peter, after some of us have tried to achieve success in some area of our life and we end up experiencing failure, we don't feel like going right back to work on it again! We get complacent when we don't see things manifesting, and walking by faith begins to seem like a far-fetched idea. We get tired and weary, and we go through the motions and obey the Word like Peter did. We know God is able to do exceedingly abundantly above all we can ask or think (see Eph. 3:20), but inside we really don't expect God to come through right away. But when we hold fast to His promises, He is faithful to perform! When you've tried already and you haven't gotten your expected end, cast your net again and experience the victory in your life!

Maybe you've been trying to win your family to Christ and it seems like you're making no progress; cast your net again! Maybe you set out to mend relationships in your life and it seems like there's no hope; cast your net again! Maybe you set out to achieve success in some personal goal or endeavor and all you've gained is discouragement; cast your net again!

When was the last time you attempted something big for God? If you want to see God begin to move in your life in unprecedented fashion, you need to cast your net again. Launch out into the deep parts. Take that new step of faith. Risk something. Be bold in your faith.

When was the last time you attempted something big for God?

When the Lord told Peter to let down his net, he didn't want to surrender. However, he did what the Lord said to do in spite of his own wants and wishes. The results were far better than he could have ever imagined! We have to cast the net. The net is not designed to be showcased on the wall of a fishing museum. Instead, we need to cast it. Let it fly! Get it out of the boat and into the water! The fishermen of Jesus' day crafted, cleaned, and mended their nets for the purpose of fishing. We must decide today what action God is requiring of us and then step out. Walk in obedience. Do what He tells us. Obey His commands. Launch out into the deep. Cast your net! The same blessings wait for you if you will do what Peter did. Jesus has spoken in His Word! Now, I ask you, will you let down your nets at the Word of the Lord?

Let us also look forward to the day we shall receive our eternal reward in Heaven. Until then, be disciplined, involved, studious, committed, full of integrity, prayerful, loving, and enduring, and you will surely live a life of a disciple of Christ who gives Him glory and impacts others just as He would want us to. You've got to do more than talk the talk. You've got to walk the walk.

Chapter 11 Review

1. Can you think of a time when you felt like giving up on having faith in God? Describe that experience.

_____

_____

_____

_____

2. Based on what you learned about the story in Luke 5:1-7, can you see the importance of trusting God's Word? List areas of your life in which you need to trust God more.

_____

_____

_____

_____

_____

_____

3. Trusting God's Word always pays off. Write down times when trusting in God's Word blessed you.

_____

_____

_____

_____

_____

4. If trusting God's Word was able to bring about those blessings, do you think He's able to do more?

_____

_____

5. In order for us to grow as disciples, we need to be able to identify things in us that keep us from having the kind of faith we should have in God. Write down things in your life that you consider hindrances to having total faith in God (i.e., fear, anxiety, people, etc).

_____

_____

_____

_____

_____

_____

6. Now that you have made a list, take these things to God in prayer and ask Him for the grace to overcome them. Once you have done this, believe that He will do it, and continue to grow in your faith. Praise Him in advance for the blessing!

_____

_____

_____

_____

_____

_____

7. Are there areas of your life that you need to cast your net again? If so, write those down and then do them.

_____

_____

_____

_____

_____

_____

Endnote

1. Pastor's Library Software, Logos Bible Software version of P. L. Tan, *Encyclopedia of 7,700 Illustrations* (Garland TX: Bible Communications, 1996).

About Calvin M. Hooper

Pastor Calvin Hooper is from Wilmington, North Carolina. He has been in ministry for almost 20 years, serving in many capacities. Pastor Hooper felt the call of God to establish a nondenominational church called the Household of Faith Christian Fellowship Church in the summer of 2003. He and his wife, Valerie, established the church and serve together in the ministry.

The Household of Faith, *aka* "The House," started with just Pastor Hooper and his family in their living room. The church is a vibrant, dynamic, growing body of growing believers, and there are plans to establish other churches.

Pastor Hooper now resides in Round Rock, Texas, with his wife and their five children, who are also very active in ministry. For more information on this ministry, visit them online at www.thehouseonline.org.

IN THE RIGHT HANDS, THIS BOOK WILL CHANGE LIVES!

Most of the people who need this message will not be looking for this book. To change their lives, you need to put a copy of this book in their hands.

> *But others (seeds) fell into good ground, and brought forth fruit, some a hundred-fold, some sixty-fold, some thirty-fold* (Matthew 13:8).

Our ministry is constantly seeking methods to find the good ground, the people who need this anointed message to change their lives. Will you help us reach these people?

> *Remember this—a farmer who plants only a few seeds will get a small crop. But the one who plants generously will get a generous crop* (2 Corinthians 9:6).

EXTEND THIS MINISTRY BY SOWING
3 BOOKS, 5 BOOKS, 10 BOOKS, OR MORE TODAY,
AND BECOME A LIFE CHANGER!

Thank you,

Don Nori Sr., Founder
Destiny Image
Since 1982

DESTINY IMAGE PUBLISHERS, INC.

*"Speaking to the Purposes of God for This Generation
and for the Generations to Come."*

VISIT OUR NEW SITE HOME AT
WWW.DESTINYIMAGE.COM

FREE SUBSCRIPTION TO DI NEWSLETTER

Receive free unpublished articles by top DI authors, exclusive

discounts, and free downloads from our best and newest books.

Visit www.destinyimage.com to subscribe.

Write to: Destiny Image
              P.O. Box 310
              Shippensburg, PA 17257-0310

Call: 1-800-722-6774

Email: orders@destinyimage.com

For a complete list of our titles or to place an order
online, visit www.destinyimage.com.